Praise for *Brilliant Selling*

A must-read for anyone aspiring to excel in sales.

Patrik Frisk, President, Timberland

Brilliant Selling is very practical and accessible, without a lot of the jargon you see in many sales books. Readers will get real and tangible value from this rich and informative book. I highly recommend it!

Paul Matthews, Managing Director, People Alchemy

I would recommend this book to anyone who wants to improve their understanding of the sales process and the art of developing and managing long-term commercial relationships, which turn into enduring partnerships.

Philip Jansen, Group Chief Executive, Brakes Group

I am really impressed with *Brilliant Selling*. I am responsible for a large corporate sales team and I have been looking for a book that will support our people. I can thoroughly recommend *Brilliant Selling* – it is full of practical tips, does not have the jargon contained in so many sales books and will, I believe, make a significant difference to both the new and experienced salesperson.

Neil Cornay, Commercial Director, L'Oréal

I put this in the top three business books I have ever read (alongside Julian Richer's excellent *The Richer Way* and Malcolm Gladwell's *The Tipping Point*). Cassell and Bird effortlessly fuse a range of techniques, templates, stories and tips into a handbook that anyone can use – whether they are an out and out salesperson, a business owner, or simply wanting to get better at influencing. You don't need to change the way you are with this book – most people are how they are. But it gives you the tools to start making small changes in the way you operate. I heartily recommend it to you, as I have to countless people personally.

Andy Coughlin, sales director and coach

Brilliant Selling is very pragmatic, which is exactly what we found when we hired Jeremy and Tom to help us improve the way we deliver sales presentations. Our salespeople and operators gained significantly from their training and coaching and we can directly link their involvement to our improved sales results.

Jeremy Alderton, Sales Director, Sodexo

Brilliant Selling: what it says on the tin – a brilliant book about selling brilliantly… a familiar friend and a refreshing change, all in one very informative and useful package. A genuine message of Doing It Right and [illegible] ernity and humanity for [illegible]

[illegible] Tribal Group

PEARSON

At Pearson, we believe in learning – all kinds of learning for all kinds of people. Whether it's at home, in the classroom or in the workplace, learning is the key to improving our life chances.

That's why we're working with leading authors to bring you the latest thinking and the best practices, so you can get better at the things that are important to you. You can learn on the page or on the move, and with content that's always crafted to help you understand quickly and apply what you've learned.

If you want to upgrade your personal skills or accelerate your career, become a more effective leader or more powerful communicator, discover new opportunities or simply find more inspiration, we can help you make progress in your work and life.

Pearson is the world's leading learning company. Our portfolio includes the Financial Times, Penguin, Dorling Kindersley, and our educational business, Pearson International.

Every day our work helps learning flourish, and wherever learning flourishes, so do people.

To learn more please visit us at: **www.pearson.com/uk**

brilliant selling

What the best salespeople know, do and say

2nd edition

Jeremy Cassell
Tom Bird

PEARSON

Harlow, England • London • New York • Boston • San Francisco • Toronto • Sydney • Auckland • Singapore • Hong Kong
Tokyo • Seoul • Taipei • New Delhi • Cape Town • São Paulo • Mexico City • Madrid • Amsterdam • Munich • Paris • Milan

This book is dedicated to our partners, Nicky and Jeanette, for their love, friendship and support.

PEARSON EDUCATION LIMITED

Edinburgh Gate
Harlow CM20 2JE
Tel: +44 (0)1279 623623
Fax: +44 (0)1279 431059
Website: www.pearson.com/uk

First edition published in Great Britain in 2009
Second edition published 2012

ISBN: 978-0-273-77120-3

British Library Cataloguing-in-Publication Data
A CIP catalogue record for this book can be obtained from the British Library

Library of Congress Cataloging-in-Publication Data
Cassell, Jeremy.
Brilliant selling : what the best salespeople know, do and say /
Jeremy Cassell, Tom Bird. -- 2nd ed.
p. cm.
Includes index.
ISBN 978-0-273-77120-3 (pbk.)
1. Selling. 2. Success in business. 3. Sales personnel. I. Bird,
Tom, 1964- II. Title.
HF5438.25.C365 2012
658.85--dc23

2012013629

10 9 8 7 6 5 4 3 2 1
16 15 14 13 12

Cartoons by Sarah Arnold
Typeset in 10/14pt Plantin by 30
Printed in Great Britain by Henry Ling Ltd., at the Dorset Press, Dorchester, Dorset

Contents

About the authors

Jeremy Cassell: I started out as a teacher when I left university. I taught English to A level, History to GCSE, ran the hockey club, coached other sports and ended up as Head of Drama at Kelly College in Devon.

After a brief spell in commercial finance, I started my formal selling career in a classic FMCG (fast-moving consumer goods) role – as a territory salesman for L'Oréal. I doubled the sales turnover in three years and even won a new Mini in a generous sales promotion! I ended up as Head of Training and Development, focusing on developing the sales force. After a brief spell at Pepsi and a management consultancy, I ended up doing what I always wanted to do – being my own boss.

So, I have been involved in selling learning, drama, hair products, crisps, consultancy, training and coaching.

I am TEFL-qualified, a certified coach and an NLP (Neuro-Linguistic Programming) trainer. I work in professional service firms, large organisations, delivering training and coaching around all areas of influencing and communication.

Outside work I play and watch a lot of sport, collect second-hand books and love spending time with my partner Nicky and our three kids (Felix, Benjamin and Isabella), who are learning how to sell all the time!

Tom Bird: I enjoyed a 15-year career in sales and business management before becoming a full-time consultant, trainer and coach. I'd like to say that the move into sales was strategic and the result of careful consideration, but in fact it was because British Airways didn't want to take someone with my poor eyesight and lack of qualifications to fly 747s (my original dream!).

Starting as a sales executive, I cut my teeth opening new accounts for measurement systems used in petrol forecourts. I moved into high-tech and software and worked with four companies over a period of 12 years in roles including Sales Manager, Sales Director, Vice-President of European Operations and Managing Director. A number of these companies started life as privately-owned US parent companies that eventually went public on the NASDAQ. This gave me broad exposure to the different challenges of private and public companies, as well as experience of sales and management in the UK, Europe and the USA.

My training, consulting and coaching work in sales is supported by a Postgraduate Diploma in Business Coaching and qualifications in Business and Finance. I am also a Master Practitioner of NLP.

Outside my work I am passionate about music (in which I have little talent), cooking (in which I have absolutely no qualifications whatsoever) and spending time with my wife Jeanette and two children Ellie and James (both of whom give me lots of opportunities to practise and improve my sales abilities!).

Training and development is our business

www.brilliant-selling.com specialises in sales training and development to meet the specific needs of modern sales professionals. We have over 30 years' experience across a wide range of organisations and work with both large corporates and SMEs. We offer bespoke in-house sales, negotiation and influencing programmes and one-to-one coaching. In addition, we are regularly invited to speak at sales conferences and offer open programmes to anyone interested in improving their skills and confidence around all aspects of selling. Contact us if you would like to find out more: jeremy@brilliant-selling.com or tom@brilliant-selling.com.

Introduction to the second edition

Welcome to the second edition of *Brilliant Selling*. We are delighted you are with us! Whatever your motives for buying this book, our intention is very simple: that *Brilliant Selling* will improve your results with practical ideas on how to sell successfully.

After a lot of soul searching we decided to write a business book back in 2007. We had a host of questions. Are we the right people? Can we write a book that will make a positive difference? Do we have enough to say? The end result was not the book you are reading! We wanted to write a book focused on sales management. It was not to be. Samantha Jackson, our commissioning editor, offered us instead the opportunity to write *Brilliant Selling* and the first edition appeared on the shelves, much to our delight, in October 2009.

We have been amazed by the response and the enthusiasm of our readers. You have told us via the Amazon five-star reviews that *Brilliant Selling* is 'almost a training manual', 'an example of the Brilliant Series at its best', 'full of very practical tips, exercises and suggestions that will have an immediate and positive impact on your selling'. In addition, the book 'hits the mark perfectly', 'simplifies how to get outstanding sales results' and 'has helped me immeasurably'. We have had numerous people connected to sales visit our website – **www.brilliant-selling.com** – and download our additional resources and complete our survey.

We are indebted to the whole team at Pearson Education who have supported us extensively and sold the rights to five countries. We have enjoyed travelling to various parts of Europe, helping with book launches. We had no idea that *Brilliant Selling* would become the number-one best-selling sales book in the UK – and we are thrilled! It has helped transform our own training and development business – we have won exciting work with new international clients and delivered numerous conference presentations on matters related to selling. On a recent trip to Hong Kong we briefly understood what it meant to be a 'G list' celebrity, having spent what felt like hours signing our books and smiling to cameras!

A lot has happened since 2009 in the world itself, as well as with selling. Anyone involved in selling will probably recognise some of these shifts:

- The modern buyer has become even more sophisticated, intolerant and price-sensitive.
- The salesperson's personal brand is becoming even more important as a differentiator.
- The importance of adding value and offering insight has become heightened.
- Cold calling is getting close to dinosaur territory.
- The old-fashioned notions of closing are no longer possible in many sales situations.

Our overriding view of this shifting sales landscape is that many of the changes are for the good and provide outstanding opportunities for outstanding people. We need to pay attention to the fundamentals like never before, which is really what *Brilliant Selling* is all about. In this second edition we have included some new information on body language and offered insights into meetings, remote sales teams, our new C^3 model (confidence, credibility and connection), and yet when we came to update the first edition we came to the conclusion that the majority of the content was still relevant and practical to all those associated with the sales process.

We would like to pay tribute to those who contributed immensely to the success of *Brilliant Selling*:

- David Cassell for his proofreading.
- Samantha Jackson for her advice and stewardship.
- Sarah Arnold for well-crafted and amusing illustrations.
- Eloise Cook and Sundus Pasha for all their help with the second edition.
- Paul Matthews and Crispin Spalding for their initial insights.
- Toby Hoskins for his improvement ideas.
- Richard Moxham for his early encouragement and advice.
- Paul Coleman for his support and guidance.

And finally, of course, thanks to all the readers who bought the first edition and influenced others to buy, and to you as a new reader if you are picking up the book for the first time. Remember to visit the website for additional resources (**www.brilliant-selling.com**) and come along to one of our open sales programmes if you can.

Jeremy Cassell and Tom Bird

March 2012

How this book works

We have all bought books that we were convinced we would read but now sit on our shelf with a corner turned in around page 27. We want **Brilliant Selling** to be different.

We talked to a lot of people involved in sales about what they would find useful and how they would like to use a book on the subject. We created a specific sales survey in which we asked over 300 successful salespeople how they sell effectively. We have used a fair amount of the evidence from this survey in the book. More can be found on our website – **www.brilliant-selling.com**.

We recognise that you may have some very specific questions about selling. These may include:

- What specifically can I do to improve my performance immediately?
- How can I sell well in an economic downturn?
- How can I make more money?
- What is current 'best practice' in selling?

With many years of sales experience behind us, we thought you would appreciate lots of academic theoretical models, impenetrable data and detailed case studies that do not relate at all to your market … maybe not! We want to focus on what works in selling. How about a book full of practical tips, war stories and exercises, based on best practice that is guaranteed to improve your results? Would that hit the spot?

We have written **Brilliant Selling** for people like you, who 'touch' selling in different ways. So, who are you?

- You work for a small or medium-sized company where everyone needs to have a basic grasp of how to sell effectively and interact with customers.
- You are either new to sales or experienced in selling and want to benchmark yourself against current best practice.
- You are involved in maximising sales performance in some way – perhaps as a sales manager, sales trainer, consultant or coach.
- You are on the periphery of sales – perhaps in a support function that touches sales, and need an understanding of the process and priorities.
- You may have 'fallen into' selling accidentally but recognise it is important as you develop your business or career.

You may also be selling to different types of customer in different markets and in different ways:

- 'Business to business' or 'business to consumer'.
- Selling a product or service – commodity or bespoke.
- Selling directly to end-users or via a distribution network.
- Selling face-to-face, online, via the telephone or some combination of these.

Whoever you are, we believe **Brilliant Selling** can help.

Who are we to write about selling?

Neither of us studied hard at school or university with the express desire of becoming salespeople. We did not dream of our perfect company car, the cut and thrust of sales meetings with customers or the feeling of euphoria that comes with achieving a sale against the odds. We are both 'accidental' salesmen.

We found ourselves in sales-related roles as much through a quirky set of circumstances as from a conscious choice.

Our sales careers have been a lot of things: enjoyable, challenging, frustrating, rewarding and, perhaps above all, self-taught. We got into sales via circuitous routes and proceeded to navigate our way through careers that were based largely on developing our own ideas of how to sell effectively. Yes, there were sales courses we attended that were helpful, but there was nothing that provided a straightforward and complete picture of what selling was and how to do it well.

Even many years into our careers there were still questions in our minds:

- Am I doing this right?
- Am I missing something?
- Is what I am doing 'good practice'?

Do you share these questions? Our intention is that **Brilliant Selling** will answer them for you!

What will work for you?

You do not have to read **Brilliant Selling** from cover to cover. You do not have to have read and understood one chapter before you can move on to the next. You don't even have to read all the chapter content to get the key points and 'best practice' tips for that topic (although it would benefit you if you did!).

So, how can you use **Brilliant Selling** to get the information that you want in the way that you want it?

- Each chapter within the book has been written so that it stands alone. It provides useful information on the topic without you needing to have read anything else in the book.
- Every chapter has a 'Brilliant Recap' at the end; this is a bullet-point list of the key points.

- Within each chapter we have put features such as quotes, exercises and key ideas. These are highlighted so that you can go straight to them.
- You can also read **Brilliant Selling** all the way through from start to finish just like a 'normal' book, of course!

What is in the book?

There are six sections, each with key specific chapters focused on different elements of selling.

The six sections are:

1. **You**. This is about you as an individual and how your personality, beliefs, values and habits impact on your sales performance. It will help you identify where to focus your efforts to improve performance.
2. **Process and planning**. It may not be why you enjoy sales but the sales process and your own planning can be critical to consistency and improved performance. We give you the key priorities.
3. **Your power to influence**. How do you build credible relationships where you can influence, communicate and negotiate with confidence? What are the core skills you need and how do you develop them?
4. **Understanding buyers and prospects**. This explains the inside track on identifying the motivations of buyers and prospects, getting the appointment and what to do in the first meeting.
5. **Presenting solutions**. This part focuses on how to get the sales result that you want from a compelling sales proposal and a persuasive sales presentation. This section will also demonstrate how to meet objections and gain agreement.
6. **Developing customers**. Once you have the sale, how do you manage customers to develop the relationship and sell more to them?

To make **Brilliant Selling** even more practical and easy for you to consume, we have included the following features:

- **Brilliant tips**: key information is summarised in the form of bullet points, making it quick and easy for you to pick up the information that will make a difference to your performance.
- **War stories**: stories help bring techniques to life and show you how they can be applied in the real world, speeding up your understanding and application.
- **Exercises**: each section has exercises that you can complete for yourself. This brings the content of this book right into your world, to help you achieve the results you want.

By purchasing this book you also have free access to the **www.brilliant-selling.com** website, which provides you with more top tips, blogs, guest contributions, case studies and additional free resources to continue your own personal sales development. This website includes an analysis of a sales survey that was completed by over 300 successful salespeople from across many markets. All you need to do is send an email to: **resources@brilliant-selling.com** to receive your exclusive free resource pack. Contact us and tell us what you think – feedback is the breakfast of champions!

Before you read on ...

Think about your goals for reading this book. What do you want to achieve specifically? What difference would it make to your job, your career and your financial success if you were even better at just one of the aspects of selling that are addressed by this book?

What if you could increase your performance as it relates to selling by even 10 or 15 per cent? What sort of impact would that have? You can start right away ... and please, get past page 27!

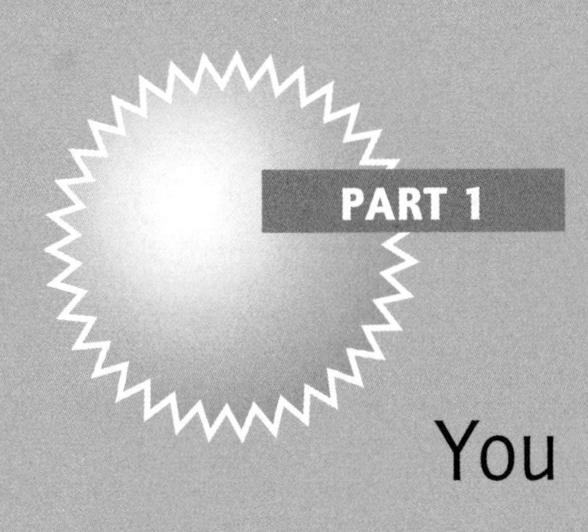

You

Have you ever surprised yourself by achieving something that you thought unlikely or even impossible?

A couple of years back I found myself in a sales situation in which I felt increasingly pessimistic about securing the order. The value of the deal was high; the competition was known to me and strong – we were the underdogs. I found myself thinking more and more about times in the past when I had lost to this competitor and 'wasted' a lot of time in the process. I finally plucked up the courage to go to my sales director and come clean about my concerns. After listening to me, he simply asked me a couple of key questions:

'Do you believe that we have the best solution for this prospect's needs?' and 'Have you asked the prospect where they see us being able to add most value to them?'

Two simple and appropriate questions that forced me to think.

I began to realise that I was losing sight of the most important thing in this deal – the value I could add and the perception of me in the eyes of the prospect. What I had done was follow a pattern that had been holding me back from winning deals above a certain value, especially when I was competing with this one specific competitor. Whenever I got an opportunity like this one I seemed to follow the same pattern of thinking, which then impacted my behaviour. What my sales director had done was raise my own awareness of this and encourage me to focus on the right things and, in doing so, to question those barriers to success that were really holding me back!

If you think about the typical salesperson, what comes to mind? A lot of people conjure up a picture of a particular type of person that they associate with a selling role. This section will answer questions including:

- Do I have the right personality to sell?
- Are there specific aspects of my personality that support or detract from my performance?
- How do my beliefs impact on my results for good or bad?
- What should I focus on if I want to improve continually?

What if you could become consciously aware of the beliefs that hold you back and do something about them? What if you could change your habitual way of communicating to more closely meet how the other person prefers to take in information? What sort of impact would that have?

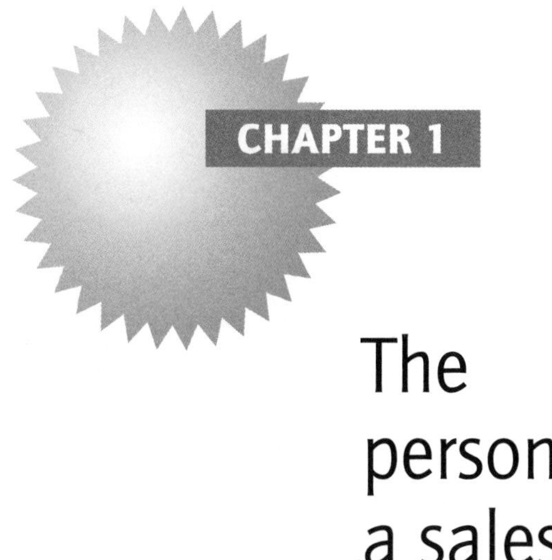

The personality of a salesperson

Most people think that all great salespeople have a certain type of personality: big, bubbly, extrovert. But one of the best salespeople that we know would certainly not describe themselves in this way. He is introverted, reserved and quiet but has one of the biggest and most powerful networks in his sector. He is a great salesperson.

Being a Brilliant Salesperson is actually about being yourself and utilising what you have to maximum effect. You may not be aware of the aspects of your own personality that support or detract from the sales results you achieve. When someone comments on some aspect of your salesmanship, what part of your personality are they focusing on?

In reality, each of us has a number of different 'personalities' that we use in different situations. We might be very different when we are alone, compared with when we are with our friends, and different again with our family or when we are at work. Are you aware of what characterises your selling personality? How do you think, act and behave when you are in the selling role?

Brilliant Salespeople do focus consciously on their personality. They identify what works and do more of it and they identify what about their personality holds them back and they change it.

> *'We are what we repeatedly do. Excellence, then, is not an act, but a habit.'* – Aristotle, Greek philosopher

Be aware of your sales persona

brilliant exercise

Think for a moment about when you last bought something of value. In addition to your desire to purchase the item, what convinced you to buy? What did you appreciate about *how* you were sold to?

Now think about a time when you wanted to buy something but chose not to because you did not like the approach of the salesperson. What was it, specifically, that you did not like?

Write down five words that describe the personality of your 'ideal' salesperson – a person most likely to make the sale to you.

Finally, as objectively as you can, write down five words that you think a new prospect meeting you for the first time would use to describe you. What might be the gaps in perception that you need to take action to close?

Are you conscious?

When we sell we often do not think consciously about how we are going to do it and whether our sales approach will help or hinder our success. We are processing so much information every second of every day that we simply have to adopt habits. Over time, these habits become unconscious – we do them without thinking.

Everyone sells differently and we need to be ourselves to sell authentically. It is no good trying to 'become' someone else when we sell. What we need to do is to consciously understand ourselves and our preferences, or habits, so that we can do more of what works and change what does not while still being ourselves! We have lots of different preferences that determine what we pay attention to, what motivates us and how we respond in a given situation.

Before we look at specific preferences let us think about how we learn and improve.

When we learn something, we go through a period of time when we have to put all of our attention on the thing we are learning – for example, riding a bicycle. After a while, this simply becomes an unconscious skill. We have developed a habit.

to create or change a habit we need three things: knowledge, desire and awareness

To create or change a habit we need three things: knowledge, desire and awareness.

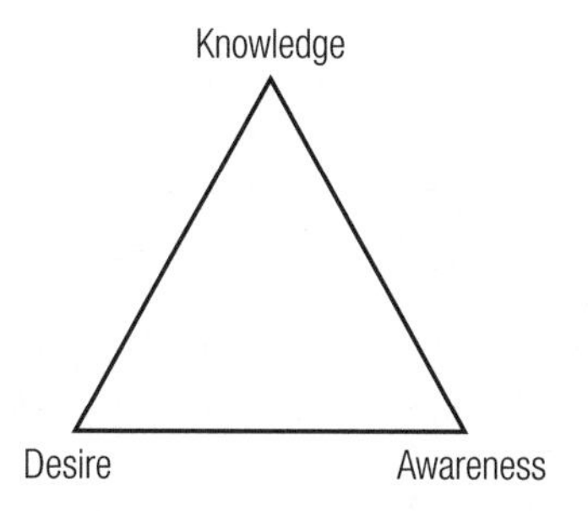

We need to be consciously aware of our existing habits if we are to change them. We need to have the knowledge of how to change (this book will help you there!) and we must have the real desire to make that change now. Some of our selling habits already support a good result and we need to be aware of these as well. The more consciously competent we are at some aspect of selling, the better we will get at it.

What are some important preferences?

Listed below are some preferences that will impact (often unconsciously) on our approach to selling. Of course, our prospects and customers will also have preferences and we will look at these in more detail in Part 3 of this book. Each preference is shown as a set of two extremes, but personality is not as clear as that. Consider each as a spectrum, with you sitting somewhere on the line between the two extremes. Some of these preferences depend on context, and so think about them relative to your selling role.

This is by no means an exhaustive list of preferences – we have just chosen three for you to consider and raise your awareness as to how they will impact on how you approach selling. As you review these three preferences, think about where you sit on the line and how these preferences influence your selling style. There are no 'rights and wrongs' to these preferences. However, being aware of yours will help you *choose* how to respond more effectively.

1 Do you take action or do you reflect?

Action ⟷ Reflector

How do you approach building a new piece of flat-pack furniture that you have bought? Do you open the box and immediately start to construct it or do you prefer to read the instructions first, maybe laying out the pieces and thinking how you will approach the task? Imagine having a strong action-oriented approach to your selling role. You are probably great at picking up the phone, arranging meetings and following through on actions.

But what about the planning aspects? Maybe you pick up the phone but have not truly thought through the right approach to take with the call. If you prefer to reflect, you are probably fantastic at thinking things through before you act. But do you put off action too long as a result? Maybe you have a very well-thought-out plan but do not always follow-through on the calls, meetings and visits necessary to turn it into success. As a person with an action preference, I know that I have learnt to be more reflective and this has helped my selling significantly. Where I used to turn up to meetings and 'wing it', I now have thought through an agenda and the possible issues that will arise.

	Action-oriented	Reflector
Strengths	Makes things happen Self-starter Wants to implement Seen by others as having 'energy' Does not avoid action	Takes time planning and thinking things through Considers the 'right' approach taking account of all the issues Gains lots of information through conversations
Warnings	May not always plan thoroughly Can be accused of 'acting first, thinking later' May irritate reflector-oriented prospects May not uncover needs as effectively as a reflector	May over-analyse at the expense of action Could irritate action-oriented prospects May miss opportunities that are time-bound

brilliant tips

If you are action-oriented, make an effort to pay attention to those aspects of selling that you might rush. They are likely to include planning for meetings, considering all the options before you propose something or take action and being extra-aware of those prospects who may be reflectors.

If you are more reflective, think about when you need to move into an action-oriented phase. Be aware of the need to take decisions with imperfect information and be especially aware when you are selling to people who are action-oriented.

2 Do you prefer detail or big picture?

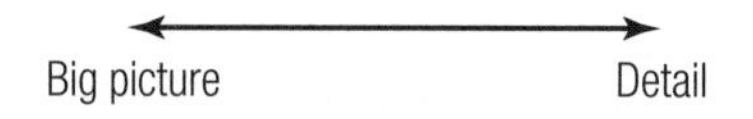

How much information do you need to feel comfortable with completing a task? Do you set headline goals or are you better at breaking these down into specific milestones?

Big-picture people prefer scope to depth. They often give an overview without the detail. I had a sales manager once who communicated a new sales strategy to me by giving me the big picture and he was completely unaware that I needed more detail – it simply was not important to him. Detail people, by contrast, prefer depth to scope. They are more comfortable with having more information about a given task. They might notice small inconsistencies that simply would not interest a big-picture person. This preference can come across in both written and verbal communication and we would do well to understand better the needs of the person with whom we are communicating. If we simply give a big-picture overview they may be left wanting more detail. If we go into small detail we may be frustrating the other person, who might merely want an overview.

The easiest thing to do is to ask how much information a person needs. If you are writing a proposal, this would be a useful thing to do! I have, in the past, sent a proposal with page after page of information and detail to someone who simply wanted a summary and some bullet points.

ask how much information a person needs

	Big-picture	Detail
Strengths	Puts things in perspective – keeps the bigger picture in mind Can see how things link together Good at giving an overview	Pays attention to important detail Comprehensive and complete in approach and correspondence Can be better at noticing risk
Warnings	Can irritate detail-conscious people May be seen as not paying attention to important detail May leave some important information out of proposals and other communications	May pay attention to unimpor-tant detail Can irritate a big-picture person with too much information May not 'see the wood for the trees' and could focus on the wrong things

brilliant tips

If you are a big-picture person, remember that some people need more information. Think about those aspects of your selling work that would benefit from a more detailed focus. These might include proposals and presentations. If you are presenting, make sure you have more detail in handouts.

If you are a detail-conscious person, make sure you pay attention to the right details. Ensure you can summarise your messages and think about using diagrams to help articulate complex ideas.

In both instances, notice what the other person needs in terms of detail. You can always ask them: 'How much detail do you need from me?'

3 Are you motivated towards something you want or away from something you do not want?

I realised, after 10 years in a variety of jobs, that I made a decision to move on, not because the new job was what I really wanted, but that it moved me away from issues and problems I was experiencing in the old job. This is very different from making choices based on knowing what you want. I went on to realise that this preference was present in a lot of decision making in which I was involved. Even if I was asked where I wanted to go to dinner by my wife I would find it easier to tell her first where I did not want to go. These are examples of 'away from' motivation. It is not wrong, it is simply more about problem avoidance than seeking a goal.

The reverse is 'towards' motivation. A friend of mine is intensely 'towards'. He does not think about problem avoidance at all. He simply considers what it is he wants and the outcome he is seeking.

Think about this preference in terms of selling to someone who is different from you. If I am 'away from', I might be positioning what I can do in terms of problems that the client will avoid. This is fine if they are similar to me but if they are 'towards' they might get frustrated at this apparent 'problem' focus. Conversely, if they are 'away from' and I am 'towards' they might see me as missing the point if they are looking to resolve issues and problems.

	Towards	Away from
Strengths	Can set compelling goals around desired outcomes Actions and milestones take you towards what you want rather than simply away from what you do not want	Motivated by avoiding problems and negative consequences Can see possible pitfalls in ideas and proposals and can look at how these can be avoided or overcome
Warnings	May not see some of the potential pitfalls to avoid with prospects May be seen as too goal-oriented by 'away from' prospects	May be so motivated by problem avoidance that there is not enough clarity about desired outcome Can be seen as 'negative' by people with a 'towards' preference May lack clear and compelling career goals

brilliant tip

When you are setting sales and career goals for yourself, make sure they are expressed in 'towards' terms – what is it that you really want rather than what are you looking to avoid or not have? By setting a 'towards' goal you know specifically where you are headed, whereas with an 'away from' goal all you know is what you will not have. Notice what motivates you and when you are using language that demonstrates this – are you making decisions to avoid something you do not want or to achieve something that you really want?

brilliant recap

Knowing more about your personality will definitely improve your selling ability. This chapter has introduced some ideas that you can explore yourself:

- There is no 'right' sales personality – people all sell differently.
- Our approach, behaviours and communication are based on unconscious preferences or habits that we have developed.
- Some of these habits support our performance and others detract from it.
- To create or change a habit we need three things: knowledge, desire and awareness.
- Knowing our preferences enables us to be flexible, to adapt in order to achieve the result we want.
- Always be aware that your way of communicating might be different from the person with whom you are communicating!

In addition to our personality, we all have beliefs and values that impact on our behaviours and results. Understanding these will help us improve our performance.

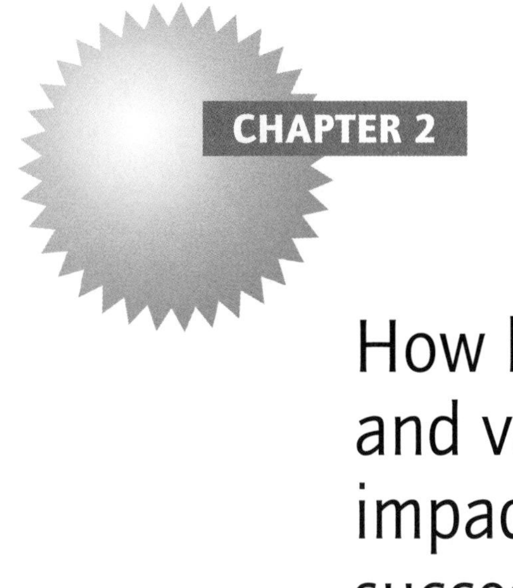

How beliefs and values impact sales success

Many years ago I went in to pitch for some business at a large international bank. At the time I was new into providing consultancy and training on a self-employed basis and, while I felt that I provided real value, I had a limiting belief about the daily rate that I could charge. A friend of mine who arranged the introduction met me in the reception area and his words surprised me. He said, 'Don't think about charging less than £2,500 per day or you won't be taken seriously'.

- What were my beliefs here?
- What were the beliefs of my friend?
- What were the beliefs of the organisation to which I was looking to sell?

Success in selling is due to much more than the behaviours and skills of the salesperson. Our decisions and motivations in selling are based on our beliefs and values. To a large extent they will determine our success.

What are beliefs and values and how are they formed?

Values

Our values are quite literally those things that are important to us, and we have values around most aspects of our life.

Some general values include:

Autonomy	*Creativity*	*Freedom*	*Trust*
Fun	*Responsibility*	*Money*	*Security*
Helping	*Respect*	*Fulfilment*	*Honesty*
Timekeeping	*Results*	*Recognition*	*Status*

Selling is no different, and we will have some specific values around that as well.

> *'Happiness is that state of consciousness that proceeds from the achievement of one's values.'* – Ayn Rand, Russian-US novelist and philosopher

brilliant exercise

Think for a moment about the job you are doing now. Answer the question: 'What do you enjoy and value about it?'. Another question to think about is: 'What's important to you about selling?'. Write down a list of words that come to mind in answer to that question. These are your values around selling.

What is in your list of values around selling? It is important to pay attention to these values and sell in a way that supports them or, at the very least, does not actively work against them. If you ignore your values you are limiting your success. Remember, Brilliant Selling is about being more of who you are, and your values are key. For example, if you value trust, it is likely that you look for opportunities to honour this value and this will support you in selling ethically. If you have trust as a value but work in an environment where it is impossible to live that value, then this will be the cause of frustration and concern to you.

if you ignore your values you are limiting your success

Does money feature in your values?

The best salespeople do have money in their values. If it is important to them, they are likely naturally to take actions that support them in realising more of it! If money is not in your list of values then take some time to consider why not, and what is in your values that can be linked with money. Having money as a value is not wrong – it enables you to do the things that you want and you can become a money magnet!

> Brilliant Selling is about being more of who you are

'We can tell our values by looking at our chequebook stubs.' – Gloria Steinem, US writer and feminist activist

Beliefs around selling and your ability to sell effectively

What are your views of used-car salesmen? My original view was that they were out to make a fast buck through smooth talking and manipulation. This view meant that for years I would not buy from independent used-car showrooms. Recently I met someone who changed my belief by providing the most professional service I had ever experienced when buying any car, let alone a used car.

- What do you think people believe about you when you sell to them?
- What are your real beliefs about selling?

If you think selling is manipulative then you are more likely to give up at the first 'no' or objection that you receive.

Beliefs are simply those things that we feel are true and they underpin our actions. They can support our sales performance or limit it.

'To succeed we must first believe that we can.' – Michael Korda, US writer and novelist

Think about this belief: 'I can't sell something that I don't believe in'.

How might this impact your performance for good or bad? The power of beliefs can be illustrated by the following example.

brilliant example

Imagine being asked to cold call for the next two weeks. How would you feel? Some of you might look forward to the opportunity but a lot of you might be saying something like: 'I could never do that!'. It is your beliefs that are driving your response. If you are saying 'I could never do that!' it is not strictly true. I mean, what would happen if you did? If cold calling was a necessary part of creating new opportunities then your belief would be limiting you. Often, if you ask someone who enjoys cold calling what they believe about it, they say things like 'It's just a numbers game', or 'The rejection is not personal', or even 'I think we have something of value to the prospect and I owe it to them to tell them about it'. Think about how the result you achieve is likely to be very different with these different beliefs.

Positive beliefs about selling will allow you to communicate passionately and convincingly. But if you do not believe in what you are selling then this is likely to come across to the other person and you are less likely to be convincing. 'What makes me believe in something?'. The answers are going to be linked closely with your values.

brilliant exercise

Ask yourself: 'What makes me believe in something that I am selling?'.

Write down the answers. These are a checklist of qualities that are important to you. How do you rank right now against each of them? What do you need to pay attention to in your selling, based on your answers?

Do your current beliefs enable you to be passionate and convincing?

So, beliefs are not *the* truth, they are just true for you. Beliefs are very personal to us – they come from friends, family, geography, and many are formed early in our lives.

> *'Myths which are believed in tend to become true.'* – George Orwell, English novelist

How can you find out your beliefs around sales and selling? Well, you can simply ask yourself what you believe and write them down.

brilliant exercise

1. Write down any beliefs around sales and selling that you hold right now.
2. Think about the beliefs that you think the most successful salesperson you know holds.
3. Notice what the differences are, if any. What beliefs do you hold about sales and selling that are holding you back? Make a list of these.

What can we do about beliefs that limit our sales success?

We now know something about beliefs. In his book *The Fifth Discipline* Peter Senge summarises William Isaacs' Ladder of Inference model to describe how beliefs are formed.

I act on my beliefs
I adopt beliefs
I draw conclusions
I make assumptions
I add meaning
I select data
Observable data and experiences

At the bottom rung we observe data – we see things as they are. Because we cannot process all the data that we receive, we make unconscious selections of the data to which we will pay attention. We then add meaning to the data that we have selected and then we make assumptions based on this meaning. We then draw conclusions based on these assumptions, from which our beliefs are formed. With every rung of the ladder we climb, we are moving further away from the objective 'truth'. By the time we have formed a belief, it is not really based on objective fact at all.

What makes this worse is that once we have adopted a limiting belief, our brain creates what is called a 'reflexive loop' that only notices information that *supports* our limiting belief. We positively sort for data that enables us to be right. So we ignore contrary evidence and we create a self-fulfilling prophecy!

The start point for changing limiting beliefs is to understand that they are not objectively true and that they also ignore other relevant information.

For each limiting belief, start looking for objective evidence to the contrary of that belief. For example, if you believe that 'Everyone I cold call feels that I am interrupting them', start looking for evidence that this is not true. It might be that you have managed to have useful conversations with some people as a result of cold calling, or even secured an appointment. Well, for these people your belief does not seem to be true. The problem with a belief is that we often discount evidence that does not support it. We are likely to say things like 'Well, that's an exception'. It also helps for us to think about the ultimate cost of holding this limiting belief. The following exercise will help to illustrate this.

brilliant exercise

Identify a belief that is limiting your sales performance now, and write it down.

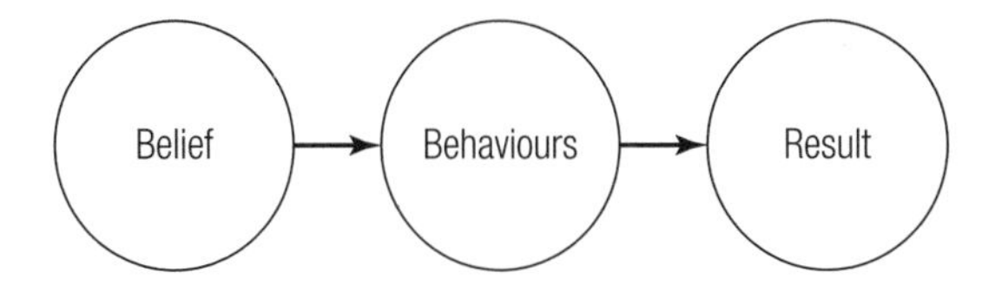

For this limiting belief, really engage with the belief and what it means. Now consider what you will be doing, your behaviours, if you are holding this belief (what you will be doing specifically, physically, mentally, etc.). Get really clear on this and write down as many things as you can think of. Finally, based on what you have written down in the 'Behaviours' step, think about what you will have as a result of these behaviours. Follow the behaviours through to their logical result. Doing this will help you realise the ultimate cost of holding the belief.

Now think about an alternative belief that you really can hold to be true. In the cold call example, instead of believing 'Everyone I cold call feels that I am interrupting them' you might be able to believe 'I have something to offer that will be of value to the people I am calling'.

With this new belief, run it through the 'Belief – Behaviours – Result' model and notice the differences.

The keys to success in changing your limiting beliefs are:

- Be aware of those beliefs that limit you.
- Think about the ultimate cost of holding these limiting beliefs.
- Think about an alternative belief that you really can hold to be true.
- Practise thinking about the new belief whenever you can and relate to the benefits of holding it.

It might surprise you how quickly the new belief becomes a habit!

brilliant recap

Your beliefs and values are at the centre of your performance. The key points covered in this chapter include:

- Our values are those things we feel are important.
- Money should be in the value set of a successful salesperson.
- Beliefs are those things we feel are true. They are formed around our values and are often not objectively true – they are just true for us.
- Beliefs can support or limit our performance.
- We can change those beliefs that limit us.

- The first step in changing limiting beliefs is to be aware of them and to realise the ultimate cost of holding them.
- Look for objective evidence to the contrary of the limiting belief – examples of when it has not been true, the exceptions.
- Think about alternative beliefs that you can hold to be true and be aware of these when you are selling.

We have beliefs and values around lots of things as salespeople, including the very purpose of our role. One aspect of Brilliant Salespeople is how they think about their role: are they simply salespeople or are they something more? Chapter 3 looks at this in more detail.

Your personal 'brand'

Many years ago I was selling software solutions to corporate users. The market was new and there were a few providers like me – some competitive technology and some complementary – serving the market. It felt like we were pioneering a new wave of technology. Each year about 35 companies like mine would embark on a roadshow around the UK and this meant we all got to know each other a little better.

It was a great opportunity for me to see all the key salespeople from the sector I was serving, both 'at work' on their exhibition stands during the day and 'at play' during the evenings and when we travelled (we were all travelling together on a couple of big coaches).

One thing became pretty clear to someone like me who was keen on observing: two or three individuals emerged as the 'go to' people in the sector. They would talk to competitors and complementary vendors alike, they seemed to have great market sector and technology understanding and they were people who seemed to be at the centre of the crowd – not necessarily taking over but always involved. On their exhibition stands they always seemed to be engaged with people – if not prospects, then other vendors and possible partners. They didn't seem to need to go looking for these people.

Fast-forward 25 years and I think you can agree that the same is true now: in any sector, niche, company or even a gathering of friends there is often at least one person who seems to influence the market, group or situation more than others. They seem to be the 'go to' people.

We can all think of some 'brands' that we are drawn to. They represent certain values that we hold as important – that seem to 'stand' for the things that interest us. We believe that now, even more than in the past, having your own personal 'brand' and becoming a 'Key Person of Influence' is an important priority for the Brilliant Salesperson.

Why is this important now?

I recently purchased a new TV system for my home and did a bit of research. When I had made my decision I asked the sales adviser who they would recommend to help with the installation and set-up. While they had a number of cards on display in their shop for freelance installers, the man I spoke to looked at me and said 'You need to speak to Luke – he will sort it all out for you', and he gave me Luke's number. Luke did not have a card on display in the store but the adviser was confident and immediate in his recommendation. I called Luke, who provided an outstanding install and set-up service. So outstanding that I have since recommended him to four of my friends (some of whom are not even looking for a new TV system!). Luke is a Key Person of Influence in his niche and local geography.

we need to be seen to be adding value

We all know that the world, the economy, our markets and our customers have changed. For most of us it is not getting easier to sell. Our customers have access to more information than ever before, markets are often more complex and so influence is less formal and straightforward, and the changing economy means we need to be seen to be adding value at every touch point that we have with a customer.

Brilliant Salespeople recognise that to succeed now requires them to extend their reach and influence beyond just having effective one-to-one conversations with prospects. They want prospects and customers – and anyone else with influence in their chosen market or niche – to be saying positive things about them. They recognise that this will help them win new prospects and customers indirectly as well as directly. Luke recognised and utilised this – and so can you in your own market and niche.

What is a Key Person of Influence?

Today's Brilliant Salesperson needs to be thought of as the 'go to' person for his or her product or service. They need to exert influence beyond just the conversations they have with individuals. They need to get those people talking positively about them to others.

In his book *Become a Key Person of Influence*, Daniel Priestly summarises some of the characteristics of a Key Person of Influence (KPI):

- Their names come up in conversation … for all the right reasons.
- They attract a lot of opportunities … the right sort.
- They earn a lot more money than most people … and it isn't a struggle.
- They can make a project successful if they are involved … and people know it.

Priestley is not restricting himself to salespeople but his observations ring true. Brilliant Salespeople focus on becoming a KPI. They are well connected, well regarded, well known and highly valued.

If you think of yourself as a salesperson you will simply act as a salesperson. In today's economy you need to think of yourself, and become, a KPI. This will lead you to taking important (but never urgent) actions that will make the difference.

What does becoming a Key Person of Influence mean in practice?

Becoming a KPI is not a set of actions you take, it is more about a way of thinking. It requires you to think of yourself differently – not just as a salesperson but more as an entrepreneur, someone who takes responsibility for their actions and their results and looks wider than just obvious sales opportunities. You are a walking, talking brand. Who do you want to attract?

In sales terms you need to be looking *constantly* for ways to become a KPI. Seven actions you can take to help become a KPI that you can definitely pay attention to as a Brilliant Salesperson include:

1. Spending time developing your knowledge and understanding of your product/service/market/prospects.
2. Being *curious* with customers and prospects – not just about how your product will work for them but asking about complementary providers with whom you can form relationships.
3. Speaking at conferences and writing papers and articles that set you apart as an expert in your field.
4. Considering your network – strategically. You have to think about who you need to network with and take steps to build the right network. Remember, networking is not about numbers as much as quality, so you must use your time wisely.

5 Thinking of ways to deliver outstanding experiences and/or service to your customers and prospects … always.
6 In every contact you have, striving to add value to the other person. Whether the other person is a prospect of your product or service or not, people recommend others who add value to them.
7 Creating your ideal introductory pitch so you can answer the question 'What do you do?' You need to think in terms of the *benefits* you bring to your customers rather than the *features* of your job. 'I help companies improve their profitability and revenues and create highly motivated sales teams' is more compelling and benefits-led than 'I design and deliver sales training'.

brilliant exercise

Take some steps to becoming a KPI in your sector and niche by spending 20 minutes considering and answering the following questions:

1 What is your ideal introductory pitch that will answer the question 'What do you do?'. Ensure this focuses on benefits rather than just a cold description of your job.
2 Take a few minutes to consider and answer the following questions as *objectively* as you can:
   - When people I have met talk about me to others, what do they say?
   - What do I *want* them to say about me?
   - What can I do immediately to help close any gap that exists?
3 What actions will you take specifically to ensure that you exceed the expectations of your prospects? What will you need to do to exceed the expectations of your customers?

brilliant recap

In this brief but important chapter we have introduced the concept of creating your own personal brand – the thing that will draw other people, including prospects, to you. This concept requires you to consider yourself, and then act to become, a Key Person of Influence (KPI).

The key points covered in this chapter are:

- In any niche, there are a few 'go to' people who exert disproportionate influence. These are the Key People of Influence (KPIs).
- Becoming a KPI requires you to think differently – not just as a salesperson but as an entrepreneur.
- KPIs become the 'go to' people for potential customers.
- Becoming a KPI requires you to spend time understanding your market and niche so that you become an expert.
- You must exceed the expectations of prospects and customers.
- You must seek to add value to *everyone* you meet so that they *want* to talk about you positively to others.

Becoming a KPI requires you to focus on developing yourself continually – and this is the subject of the next chapter.

Performance and selling

Imagine this scenario for a moment. You have just finished a lengthy sales meeting with your boss. You have been left in no doubt that you have to hit the quarterly revenue target. He is under pressure and, therefore, so are you. In fact, you spent most of the meeting discussing the revenue number and the prospects and whether one prospect was 80 per cent likely to close this quarter or 70 per cent likely. The discussion was about the ranking and the likelihood of the deal closing. Sound familiar? This is a meeting about 'results'.

It is often said that 'sales is all about results'. In a real way this is true, of course. The only problem is, we cannot 'do' a result. If the sole focus of our attention is the number, the target, or sector penetration percentage then we might know when we have got there (because it is likely to be measurable) but achieving the objective is dependent upon our **performance** – those things that we can control and do, which either contribute or detract from our achieving the result.

Contrast this with a meeting that outlines the result (you need to hit the number) and then discusses your specific action plan for each account. Maybe for one the focus is on the next meeting and how you can plan and prepare. Maybe for another it is brainstorming how you can reach the decision maker and what might influence them the most. This latter scenario is focusing on different aspects of performance that will then help maximise the chance of achieving the result or objective that you want.

'A bad manager confuses activity with performance.' – Anon

What makes a focus on performance so effective is that *you are in control of it*. Think about an Olympic swimmer training for the 400m freestyle event. Clearly the result he/she will want is to win the event. But the swimmer cannot control that outcome because there are seven other swimmers in the same pool. The swimmer must therefore set a performance goal which acts as the focus.

keep focused on only those things that you can control or influence

A number of things contribute to performance in sales and you need to keep focused on only those things that you can control or influence. For most people, the following diagram helps illustrate what these components of performance are.

The performance iceberg

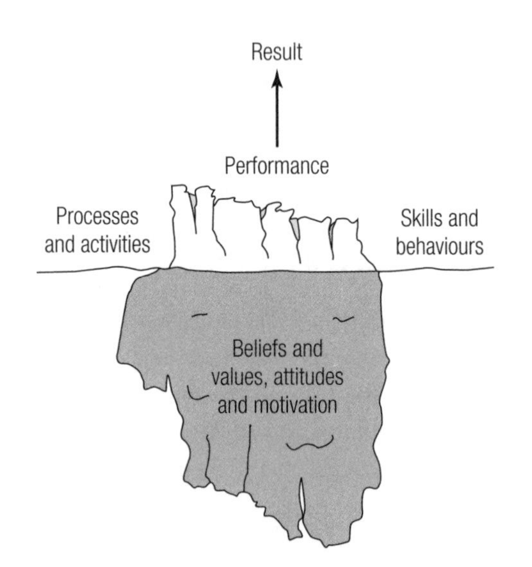

The visible things that contribute to our sales performance (i.e. those things that are above the surface and can be observed) are the processes and activities we follow and the skills and behaviours we demonstrate and use.

Processes and activities

Selling requires a process to sit behind it. Without a process we cannot manage the different aspects of the sale and, therefore, our performance in each aspect. We may have preferences for certain parts of the sales process, and monitoring our activities and the process steps we follow is a quick way to start improving our performance immediately.

We cover the sales process in detail in Part 2 but some specific aspects of performance on which we can focus, in terms of process and activities, include:

- Do we pay equal attention to each stage of the sales process or focus on one to the exclusion of others?
- Do we make enough calls to new prospects to get the meetings we require?
- Do we always follow up after sending a quote or proposal?
- Do we ensure that we update the records after each call?

Skills and behaviours

In carrying out sales process steps and activities we use a variety of observable behaviours and skills to help achieve a result. A number of these are covered in Part 3 and they include:

- The extent to which we build rapport (a harmonious connection) with the other person.
- Our ability to use effective questioning to uncover buyer needs.
- Our ability to influence the buyer to see the benefits of the product or service we are selling.

- Our effectiveness on the telephone to secure a meeting.
- The way in which we conduct our meetings, including how much we speak relative to the prospect.

Like all good icebergs, only the tip is visible and a great deal more exists beneath the surface. We cannot see these things directly but we can definitely see the impact of them.

Beliefs and values

An awareness of our beliefs and values helps us understand certain patterns of behaviours and results that we achieve. For example, if we believe that we cannot cold call, it is likely that we will avoid that activity. No amount of skills or process will help!

Attitude

This is another very important but often unseen contributor to sales performance. What is our attitude to dealing with clients? What about our attitude to work generally? When a customer requests more information and perhaps does this more than once, what is our attitude towards them? We are in control of our attitude and it is something of which we need to be aware.

> we are in control of our attitude

Motivation

What gets you up in the morning? It is our motivation that provides the energy for our work and it is often linked with our values. For example, sometimes when I need a bit more motivation to go the extra mile, I think about the great family holiday that I am planning and for which I need the money!

Taking control

If you are serious about improving your performance, you need to look at each of these areas objectively and take action where required.

brilliant exercise

Use the template in the free resource pack (email **resources@brilliant-selling.com** to receive this pack) or create your own to list objectively the following:

1. What are the key results on which I am judged (sales revenues, margin, new clients, etc.)?
2. Process/activities: being objective, what are the process steps or activities in my selling that I do not focus on enough?
3. Skills/behaviours: reflect on the last two weeks and think about the skills and behaviours you use in your daily sales work. Use the list below as a start point and add your own skills/behaviours to it:
   - Building rapport.
   - Questioning skills.
   - Listening skills.
   - Talking about benefits rather than features.
   - Taking time to uncover needs before trying to present products.
   - Offering insight.

Prioritise the list in terms of where your efforts on developing the skill/behaviour will have most impact. Write down specific actions for the top three and remind yourself to do these (put in your diary a reminder to focus on preparing three great questions before each meeting every day, for a week, for example). Better still, seek objective feedback from a colleague or manager on what your priorities should be.

Print this out and add to it – make it a regular source of your personal reflection and it will pay dividends.

A final warning about a focus exclusively on results is illustrated with this story. Years ago, I was selling consumer products to retail outlets. I had been having a good year but was slightly behind on the current quarter. If I could hit that quarter I would get a bonus and my sales manager kept reminding me of it and encouraging me to push for every sale I could. I went into one outlet where I had developed a good relationship with a customer and, with my sales manager's results-focused words in my mind, I managed to sell a significant amount of product for them to stock. I was happy. I had hit my quarterly number and made my bonus. Unfortunately, the customer could not sell the product and it was the last time they bought from me. I had sacrificed the relationship and future sales for that one result.

One thing we have not discussed here but that is very relevant to performance is the setting of specific and appropriate goals. We cover this in detail in Part 2 on planning. We would encourage you to apply the principles detailed there to your own personal performance in terms of behaviours, skills, activities and processes. More information on this can be found on the **www.brilliant-selling.com** website and by using the templates contained in the free resource pack (which you can receive by sending an email to **resources@brilliant-selling.com**).

Awareness and responsibility – the keys for continual improvement

Everything we have talked about in this chapter requires you to put your attention on those aspects of what you do – your performance – that contribute to achieving a result. This brings us to a key point about improving performance. There are two things that you must have to bring about any change in behaviour (or belief): **awareness** and **responsibility**.

The performance iceberg gives labels to different aspects of performance but it all comes down to these two words.

Awareness

I can only change a behaviour or belief if I am first aware of what I am doing. Sounds obvious, but we all do things of which we are not consciously aware. If we are not aware of them we cannot change them. Take an example of someone who seems consistently to get to the stage of making a proposal but not winning the business. They think they are doing everything right until one helpful prospect gives them feedback on why they lost the deal: 'The other suppliers asked questions that uncovered our real business needs. You had a good product but we did not feel you fully understood our challenges'. Some salespeople would simply listen to the feedback, put it down to experience and go on to the next opportunity, choosing not to learn from the experience. A Brilliant Salesperson would ask more questions and raise their awareness on an aspect of their performance that is limiting his result. The Brilliant Salesperson might choose to change their approach with the next prospect and, whatever the outcome, seek feedback on that aspect of his work – possibly by bringing a colleague in to observe.

The great news is that as soon as you put your awareness on something, your performance on that aspect of your work automatically and unconsciously improves! Imagine that! Putting an aspect of your performance under the magnifying glass improves it almost without trying. Think back to learning how to drive a car. The first few times, you try to pull away smoothly and find the right balance between letting out the clutch and depressing the accelerator may not have been as smooth as you would have liked. But, in a remarkably short period of time (hopefully), by putting your attention on it you simply improve naturally and easily.

Responsibility

This can be written another way: response-ability. In order to take responsibility for your own performance you need to realise that you have a response-ability, a choice of how you act and respond in any given situation. Remember, we work largely from unconscious habits and so we need to think about our actions if we are to see that there are other ways of responding. If, as has been my habit in the past, I consistently created quotations with lots of detail but without summarising the key and compelling reasons why the customer should buy from me,

I do have a choice to change it if I want. I might ignore regular feedback from colleagues, justifying my action in any number of ways, but I do have a choice.

brilliant tips

- Seek objective feedback from your prospects, clients and colleagues. Challenge them to be specific about what they observe and what you could do differently.
- Really practise noticing the impact of everything you do – especially the conversations you have with clients and prospects.
- When you do not get the result that you want, think about what other choices you have so that you can respond differently next time.

brilliant recap

The key points covered in this chapter concerning performance are:

- A focus on performance and not just results will bring about the improvements you want.
- Performance is made up of visible processes, activities, skills and behaviours, as well as often-invisible beliefs, attitudes and motivations.
- Your beliefs, attitudes and motivations have a bigger impact on your performance than the visible components.
- The two keys to improving performance are responsibility (response-ability) and awareness.
- Bringing your awareness to something automatically improves your performance.

Performance is something that we can control, develop and improve. One great way to do this continually is through self-coaching, and this is the topic of the next chapter.

Continually improving through self-coaching

Brilliant Salespeople engage in self-coaching all the time – even if they do not call it that.

Coaching has emerged in recent years as a popular development tool. While it came from the world of sport, its application and success in business relates to its focus on increasing responsibility and awareness. Many businesses employ coaches to help senior managers, but coaching is also something that you can use very effectively on yourself.

Some of you will have a sales manager and others will not. Even if you do report to a sales manager the chances are that you are, to a large extent, left to your own devices. You need to achieve the sales result with limited input and support from your colleagues. The previous chapter talked about the importance of awareness and responsibility in improving performance and, therefore, the result you achieve. For most, this improvement in performance is largely going to be down to you. So, you need to learn how to self-coach.

> *'Five frogs are sitting on a log. Four decide to jump off. How many are left? Answer: five. Why? Because there's a difference between deciding and doing.'* – Mark L. Feldman and Michael F. Spratt, *Five Frogs on a Log*

The intention with your self-coaching is to raise awareness and response-ability through reflecting on what it is that you do. There are primarily two uses of self-coaching that the Brilliant Salesperson focuses on: general development leading to continuous improvement, and specific development of a skill or ability.

raise awareness and response-ability through reflecting on what it is that you do

General development leading to continuous improvement

This involves creating the habit of reflecting – often at the end of each day or after a sales call or other meeting. The intention is to become much more aware objectively, of, how you perform. This requires you asking questions and taking the time fully to consider the answers, noticing and challenging any assumptions.

Two examples of how you can use this to improve are:

After a sales meeting with a prospect or a customer

Take a few minutes immediately after you finish the meeting (resist the urge to put it off until later – do this while the meeting is still fresh in your mind) to ask yourself some key questions on different aspects of the meeting, so that you can become more objectively aware of how you performed. These questions might include:

- Did I meet my objective for the call? If not, what specifically could I have done, in hindsight, to have improved my chances?
- Considering my planning of the meeting, to what extent was my goal for the meeting appropriate and realistic? What could I have done in my planning to have improved the outcome?
- What did I do well in the meeting?

- What have I learned from the meeting about my approach, skills and behaviours?
- What did I do, specifically, that moved the relationship forward?

At the end of each day

Take five minutes at the end of every day to reflect on the day and your performance. Developing this habit is probably the quickest way to improve your abilities and success. Questions that you can ask here include:

- What did I do really well today?
- What is one thing that I have learned from today?
- What will I do differently in future as a result of today?

Specific development of a skill or ability

When you have identified a particular skill or activity that you want to improve, then you can focus your self-coaching on this. The process is the same as for general development but with the addition of some specific goals, which you set for yourself in advance, around the skill or activity.

An example of this might be your ability to establish the right first impression.

First of all, you need to define what the 'right' first impression is that you want to create. It may be that this relates to establishing credibility early on with the prospect. This may require you to know something about their business and that you show this in the first five minutes of the conversation with them. You might then want to consider how well you think you are doing at this right now. On a scale of 1–10, where 10 is 'totally credible', where do you think you are now? Where do you want to be on this 'credibility with my prospects' scale in, say, two months? Once you have a specific goal you can then hold the meeting and reflect on how well you did. Questions you might ask yourself after the meeting in this example include:

- What did I do to establish credibility in the meeting and when did I do this?
- What was the impact of this that I observed in the prospect (what did I see and hear)?
- Did the behaviour achieve the objective as far as I can tell? If not, what could I do more of/less of/differently next time?

making self-coaching a personal habit will dramatically improve your performance

Making self-coaching a personal habit will dramatically improve your performance – all for an investment of five minutes a day! Why would you not do this?

Feedback from colleagues

If self-coaching is something that you can choose to do every day, without needing the support of anyone, then seeking opportunities to get feedback from your colleagues or sales manager is something you should do whenever you can.

It is surprising how little feedback we get that we can use to our benefit. Often this is because the person giving the feedback has not been trained on how to give effective feedback. Great feedback is both objective and specific. Feedback such as 'You did really well in that meeting' is next to useless. Feedback such as 'You really engaged the prospect around how we could help him' is better but still lacks the specifics that make it really useful. Feedback such as 'When you asked questions about his business and then linked our product to solving his biggest problem' is much better because it tells you specifically what it was you did that was good. This is the same for feedback on those things you want to improve. A colleague giving feedback such as 'At the start of the meeting I noticed that you asked two questions [gives you examples] and when the prospect didn't answer immediately you gave him two alternative answers' is much more useful than 'You need to work on your questioning skills'.

The point here is that it is up to *you* to ask for the feedback you want from your colleagues or manager. Do not assume that a) they will give it to you at all and b) they know how to give you great feedback.

If you get an opportunity to be accompanied during your sales activities at any time, then decide the specific areas on which you would value feedback. Ensure that you get specific, observable, objective feedback. This kind of feedback is a real gift. Truly objective feedback from someone other than yourself can make a real difference to your awareness and performance.

> *'You cannot teach a man anything. You can only help him discover it within himself.'* – Galileo, Italian astronomer

brilliant recap

Self-coaching is guaranteed to improve your sales performance. In this chapter we have discovered:

- Brilliant Salespeople self-coach and it takes only five minutes a day.
- Self-coaching raises your awareness through asking good open questions about your own performance and reflecting objectively on the answers.
- You can use self-coaching for general development (by reviewing your day) or to develop specific skills.
- Seeking feedback from colleagues is another way to help coach yourself.
- Be explicit about what feedback you want and ensure it is both objective and specific.

One really important facet of sales that we can focus time and attention on is the sales process and our own preparation. This is covered in the next section of this book.

PART 2

Process and planning

I attended a meeting with a prospect some years ago. I arrived at her office with very little time to spare (because I had not planned my journey or the time it would take) and spent a few rushed minutes in the car preparing an agenda (which I should have sent in advance). When I did meet the prospect, I had not planned any of my questions and so failed to drive the meeting in the way that I needed. I did not get the business!

I also remember managing a sales team in which I had two very different individuals. One spoke to lots of prospects, submitted lots of proposals and won a good deal of business. He succeeded through working very hard and having so many prospects that in any given month a number would buy from him. But, he never really knew who it would be. He was spinning a number of plates and putting his attention on the ones most likely to fall rather than planning a systematic approach to achieve the result he wanted. The other salesperson had fewer prospects but would know very specifically where they were in the sales process and what her next step was. Her accuracy was impressive and she always seemed to make her long-term forecast. When you are managing a business, predictability is absolutely critical and I came to value her accuracy very highly. Over time, because she had knowledge of her prospects and where they were in the sales process, we could work to improve her results.

The first story is about planning and the second is about process. When we were researching this book we were looking for some inspirational quotes for each section and it became apparent that there were not many inspirational quotes concerning process and planning! It is fair to say that a lot of salespeople do not enjoy or see the value of a focus on process and planning. While the words 'process' and 'planning' might not be synonymous with inspiration, they are critical within the context of Brilliant Selling. Process and planning done well:

- Underpin and provide structure to all the activities that you carry out towards achieving your desired result.
- Help keep the real priorities in the front of your mind.
- Ensure that you get the best possible result from the activities in which you engage.

This section will answer questions including:

- What are the key stages of the sales process, why are they important and what are my priorities in each?
- How do I make the most effective use of my time?
- What aspects of my work will really benefit from time spent on planning?
- What sales-related information should I pay attention to and how can it help me achieve the results that I want?

A focus on process and planning takes relatively little time but it is often the difference between consistency in your selling and the stressful cycle of 'feast or famine' in sales results that some people experience. It is a big differentiator in Brilliant Salespeople.

The sales process as a tool for improvement

We all do things every day that involve process, including cleaning our teeth and getting ready for work. Some of these processes we do well and some not so well.

brilliant definition

Process can be defined as 'a series of actions or steps in making or achieving something', and it implies progress towards a desired end result.

Whatever you sell, it is likely that there will be a series of steps that you can, or do, follow that take you from an initial conversation with a prospect through to the closing of a sale. There may be some specific nuances and process steps, depending on the nature of your market, product, service and purchaser. In this chapter we share with you a simple sales process that can be applied in a wide variety of sales environments. We encourage you to use it as a tool to raise your awareness as to where you can better spend your time to develop the results that you want, knowing that there may be some adaptation required on your part.

What's the point?

This is something that I have heard from salespeople in the past. They say things such as 'You can't put what I do into a simple process' and 'Every sale is different'. These comments may be true to some extent, but the main benefit of having and following a sales process is that we can monitor and measure our performance in each step. This enables us to focus on developing better results at each stage of the process, thereby improving our sales and our consistency.

'Success is a process more than a realisation.' – Anon

This diagram summarises the seven steps of the 'generic' sales process. Through all the steps runs the thread of establishing and building connection and credibility. The fact is that you need to demonstrate these at every step of the sales process. We discuss connection and credibility in Part 3 of this book.

In this section we look at each step of the process and provide a summary of what the step involves, what some of the common problems or issues experienced in that step are and what your key priorities should be.

1 Prospect

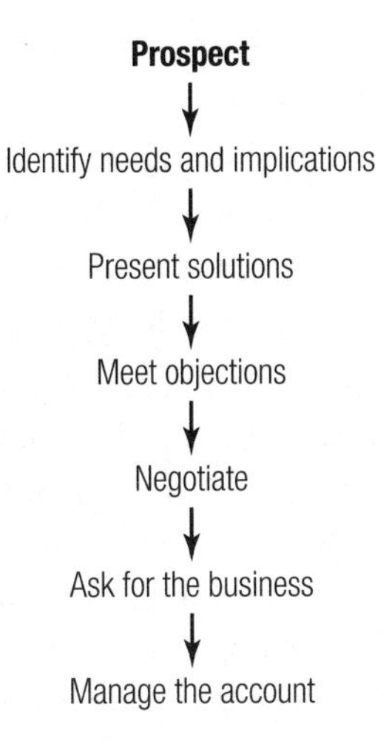

While different definitions of prospecting exist, our view is that the term encompasses all of the activities related to defining, targeting and developing prospects for your product or service. For most salespeople, if you do not spend enough time prospecting you can easily run out of customers. Even when times are good we need to fill the funnel with new prospects so that customers continue to buy from us.

What does it involve?

- **Identifying possible prospects**: before you can attract prospects, you need to identify a prospect profile. There will be a number of questions depending on your situation and market but they are likely to include variations of the following:
  - Who, specifically, will buy from me?
  - Why, specifically, will they buy from me?
  - Where, specifically, will I find them?
  - How, specifically, will I know them from other people who are less likely to buy from me?

Do you notice a theme in the questions? That word 'specifically' is critical to answer. The tighter we can define our prospects the more focused and successful our sales efforts are likely to be.

- **Targeting possible prospects**: having identified possible prospects we need to target them effectively. What is the best way for them to receive a compelling message about what we are offering that enables us to start a dialogue?
- **Developing prospects**: we need to qualify them in or out of our sales process. We need to make a decision on how likely they are to buy from us. Above all, we need to be objective at this point. It is easy to fool ourselves into thinking that everyone we talk to represents a possible sale, but if we do not qualify objectively we waste time that could be spent with people who are more likely to buy! We need to establish qualification criteria – aspects that we know to be true or untrue for most people who would buy from us.

What are some common problems?

- **Not being really clear on the prospect profile**: we waste time talking to people who may be unlikely or unwilling to buy.
- **Being clear about our prospect profile but not acting on it**: we may engage in activities with people that we know are unlikely to buy from us.
- **Not doing enough activity**: when sales are good we might 'ease off' on prospecting activity. This leads to a 'feast or famine' result.
- **Not qualifying early enough**: if we do not qualify our prospects objectively we will have too many people going through the other stages of the sales process and will not be able to manage them all effectively. It is far better to put fewer prospects through into the sales pipeline but know they are the right ones to spend your time on!

make sure you engage in enough prospecting activity

What are your key priorities?

- **Make sure you engage in enough prospecting activity**: you must make time for prospecting if you are to achieve consistent sales results. It is not simply something to do when the sales are not coming in.
- **Be objective in your qualification of prospects**: be realistic and make decisions on objective criteria.

Outcome

The outcome from this first stage of the sales process is qualified prospects who enter the sales pipeline to be managed through the other steps of the sales process.

Part 4 of this book is focused on prospecting and will give you more detail on this important aspect of Brilliant Selling.

2 Identify needs and implications

This step in the process is about discovery. The key skills that you use will be questioning and listening. Before somebody makes a decision to buy something they need a good reason. The product or service will either do something that they want or it will prevent something that they do not want. In either case, the reasons for taking the action you want them to take must outweigh the reasons for inaction. They need to see the **value** in what you are offering.

You need to take the time to understand fully their needs and, through further questioning, help them see the implications of these needs, if they are not met.

What does it involve?

- **Discovery**: finding out more about the prospect and their specific needs through questioning and listening skills.
- **Building the motivation to make a buying decision**: asking more questions will help turn a need into something that motivates the person to take action – to want to buy. They need to see the benefits of taking action.

What are some common problems?

- **We do not ask enough questions**: we move too quickly into discussing our product or service and we cannot link it effectively with the prospect's needs or give them a big enough reason to take action.
- **We make assumptions**: we think we know what they need and what is important to them so we either do not ask or we ask closed questions, which may reduce our connection and credibility with them.

What are your key priorities?

- **To understand fully their needs**: this will enable you to personalise how you present the solution to them in the next stage of the process.
- **To have helped them build a compelling reason to take action**: they must be motivated to act *before* we position our product or service to them.

Outcome

A motivated prospect who understands why they need to take action.

Part 3 of this book looks in more detail at the skills of questioning, listening and needs analysis.

3 Present solutions

Presenting your solution involves building a compelling case that confirms why *your* solution is the ideal fit for the prospect and their needs. It is important at this stage to consider things from the prospect's perspective rather than your own. This stage may be part of the same discussion as the needs identification or it might be a separate meeting or discussion. The key skill here is influencing, and you can only influence effectively if you have all the facts from the prospect to form the basis for your presentation.

What does it involve?

- **Articulating benefits**: being clear on how your product or service answers the prospect's needs specifically.
- **Gauging their reaction objectively**: so that you can assess their interest and identify what you need to focus on.
- **Providing a written proposal**: in some cases this might be necessary and could be either a formal proposal or something more succinct.
- **Presenting**: you may need to present to an individual or to a group.

What are some common problems?

- **We make assumptions**: assumptions might include that the prospect knows why our product or service is the best, that we know what is important to them and that we know how they buy this type of product or service.
- **We communicate features**: we present what the product or solution does rather than how it benefits the prospect.
- **We do not present to the right person(s)**: we do not take account of other decision makers or possible steps in the buying process.

What are your key priorities?

- **Articulate the benefits in the prospect's terms**: use their words from the identifying needs phase to link your product or service to their requirements.
- **Uncover** any additional steps or information needed to progress the sale.
- **Influence the decision maker**: so that the value or benefit of your product or service outweighs the 'cost' of doing nothing (this might be in emotional or hard business terms).

articulate the benefits in the prospect's terms: use their words

Outcome

A buyer convinced of the benefits of your product or service and identification of what you need to do in order to close the sale.

Presenting solutions is covered in more detail in Part 5 of this book.

4 Meet objections

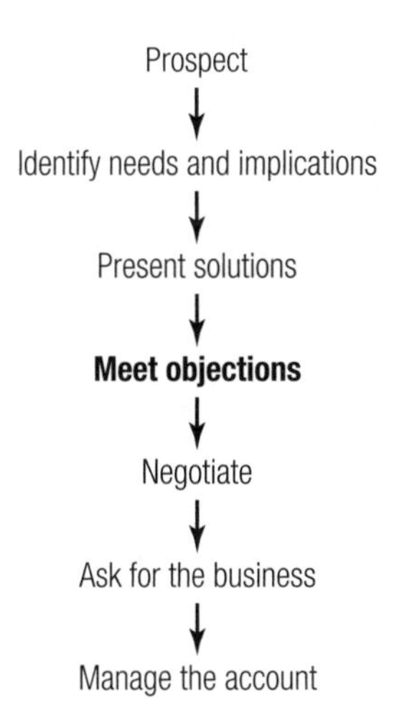

A lot of sales training courses talk about 'overcoming' or 'busting' objections, but this implies they are barriers rather than enablers to your sale. An objection is often simply a request for more information. Objections are a natural part of the sales process and they show the prospect is interested and considering how they could take your product or service forward.

What does it involve?

- **Surface and welcome objections**: if you do not surface objections you cannot handle them effectively.
- **Fully understand them**: you will need to ask more questions to understand the objection clearly.
- **Address them correctly and fully**: you need to take the objections seriously and make sure you answer them.
- **Check with the prospect**: do not move on until you know the prospect is satisfied that the objection has been addressed.

What are some common problems?

- **We avoid objections**: we might fear them and so try to avoid dealing with them.
- **We do not deal with them effectively**: we give an answer but do not check that it has truly addressed the prospect's concerns.

What are your key priorities?

- **To welcome objections**: how you feel about objections will impact on how you handle them. Think of them as requests for more information.
- **To take the time to address them**: address them fully and not with a cursory answer that you think might do the job.

- **Not to move on before you know they have been addressed**: unless you address the objections the prospect will still have doubt in their mind – moving on too quickly will reduce your chance of making the sale. You need to test whether an objection has been satisfactorily resolved.

Outcome

The prospect is left with no substantive reason not to buy. You are free to start the negotiation and asking-for-the-business stages with no outstanding issues (other than terms).

Part 5 of this book covers objections in more detail.

5 Negotiate

Technically, negotiation is not something you aim to do as part of the sales process. This might sound strange but the ideal is to have the prospect emotionally bought into your product or service before you start negotiating. If they have agreed, in principle, to buying, then the negotiation is about the terms. If you negotiate too early, it can link the purchase **decision** to the terms, making it likely that you will need to discount or make other concessions.

What does it involve?

- **Reaching agreement on the terms**: terms can encompass many things other than price; negotiation relates to gaining agreement on the total package (whatever that might be).
- **Trading concessions**: to agree terms you may need to give something to the prospect (an increase in payment terms, for example). In return for this you would ask the client for something (to commit to purchasing a certain quantity, for example).

What are some common problems?

- **We assume we will need to negotiate**: this leads us to talking discounts before they are requested. Salespeople can be far too accommodating!
- **Thinking it is *all* about price**: do not deduce their intentions from your fears – buying is often not about price but emotion.
- **Not linking the product to the value it brings for the prospect**: we constantly need to make this link and not get into discussing terms in isolation of what the purchase will bring the customer.
- **Giving rather than trading**: we may give in to requests for discounts or better payment terms without asking for something in return. This can set a precedent in the relationship.

What are your key priorities?

- **To reach an agreement that works well for both parties**: not one that just works for you *or* the prospect.

Outcome

The way is now clear to secure the sale.

Negotiation is covered in more detail in Part 3 of this book.

6 Ask for the business

If you do the other stages of the sales process well, with connection and credibility throughout, this is the easy part. The main point here is actually to ask for the sale.

What does it involve?

- **Check that you have met all of the objections**: before you ask for the order it makes sense to check that all the prospect's questions have been addressed to their satisfaction.
- **Choose how best to ask for the sale**: think about what would work most effectively.
- **Ask!**

What are some common problems?

- **We might put off asking**: we may not feel comfortable asking for the sale and this might lead us either to put off asking for the sale or make our request sound more like an apology.
- **We might ask too early**: if we ask before we have met all objections we might get a 'no'.

What are your key priorities?

- **To consider when to ask and how to ask.**
- **To gain commitment!**

Outcome

A sale is secured in which all parties win.

Gaining commitment and closing the deal is covered in more detail in Part 5 of this book.

7 Manage the account

For some of you each sale will be to a new customer, but for a lot of people selling is about creating a relationship that might lead to more than one sale. If this is the case for you, then managing the customer relationship is an important stage of the sales process. It is five times easier to sell to an existing customer than to win new ones and so it is well worth the effort maintaining good relations.

What does it involve?

- **Focus on the relationship**: if a customer feels you are only interested in making a sale, they are unlikely to see value in the relationship and may well go elsewhere in future. Stay in touch as regularly as is appropriate. Make sure you know the right people in the customer's business, and form relationships to help develop your position.
- **Look to add value and insight**: how you do this will differ depending on your market, but successful account managers look to add value to their customers whenever they can.

What are some common problems?

- **Not making time for it**: this is an important task but never urgent, so we often focus on other things.
- **Focusing on only one person**: we leave ourselves exposed if we focus on just one person. What if they leave? Where is our relationship then?

What are your key priorities?

- **Develop the relationship to greater levels of trust**: we need to set goals around developing the relationship so that we erect barriers for the competition and maximise the chances of future business.

Outcome

This might differ depending on your particular situation but ideally the outcome should be a broad and deep customer relationship built on trust, which will yield additional sales.

Managing the customer is covered in more detail in Part 6 of this book.

brilliant recap

Having and following a simple sales process is good for our results. While the specific process that you follow might have some differences from the process we have covered here, the key points are:

- Having well-defined steps in a sales process enables you to monitor and measure your performance in each step more objectively, thereby improving your performance and consistency.
- Connection and credibility are needed by Brilliant Salespeople at every step of the sales process.
- Our tendency to make assumptions is a common problem for salespeople at each step of the process – we need to seek objectivity to improve performance.

Once we have a well-defined sales process to follow, we all need to make choices about how we spend our time in order to be most effective in our role. This is covered in the next chapter.

CHAPTER 7

Making the most of your time

One thing that we often hear from salespeople is that there is never enough time to do everything. In sales, there are always more things that we can do: more prospects to call, more customers we could visit, more administration that we could complete. One of the big issues that Brilliant Salespeople have mastered is how to make the very best use of their time. They know where to spend time for the greatest return and they do not confuse activity with results.

do not confuse activity with results

Time is one of those things that is finite. We cannot change it. The very best that we can do is to understand where we spend our time now and consider if it is on the right things. Our habits, combined with external and internal pressures, lead us to spending time on some activities at the expense of other activities. Having made some decisions on what the 'right things' are, we can then choose to change our habits to ensure that these right things get done.

'Time is money.' – Benjamin Franklin, US statesman

What can you control?

In his book *The 7 Habits of Highly Effective People*, Stephen Covey details what it is that effective people seem to do habitually. One of these habits is that effective people focus their time only on those things that they can control or influence. If you think about it this is common sense, but how often have you found yourself fretting or spending time worrying about things that you can do nothing about? The Brilliant Salesperson recognises when they are doing this and they stop. He or she focuses on an aspect of the situation over which they have some influence. For example, in an economic downturn it is easy to focus a lot of time worrying about how bad things are and how competitors are hungry for the business that you are also chasing. If you ask yourself what you can control about the situation, you might realise that the economy is the same for everyone and that your efforts are best placed deepening prospect and existing customer relationships. This activity might develop more of a competitive edge for you. While this approach will not make the problem go away, it does put you in a stronger situation because you are choosing to focus on something you can action.

spend your time on those things that you can impact and change

brilliant tip

For any problem that you find yourself facing, ask yourself 'Over what aspect of this problem or issue do I have some control or influence?' and focus your time on that aspect. If you have no control, then move on and spend your time on those things that you can impact and change.

What are the 'right' things?

Once we have made a commitment to focus only on things we can control, we can turn our attention to the choices we are making. Where do we spend our time now? Often, we spend time on those things we are good at or enjoy. We also spend time on things that we are pressured to do by others. Over time it is easy to become reactive and not make conscious choices over the things on which we focus time and attention.

With limited time and a need to maximise our effectiveness and performance we need to make conscious choices. But how? And if we are not doing the right things now, how will we make the time for them? It is not as if we have lots of spare time to fill!

it is not the activity that counts, it is the result you achieve

We have to start by questioning our prioritisation. In addition to making choices based on what we prefer to do, we are likely to be responding to things we perceive as being urgent. But these are not necessarily going to move our sales forward. Things that move sales forward are important and not necessarily urgent. Some examples of important, but not urgent, things include:

- Reflecting on our performance at the end of each day to define what worked well and what we will do differently tomorrow.
- Planning an agenda for a prospect meeting.
- Researching a prospect's company so that we know more about their business.
- Setting specific goals around a stage in the sales process where we know we need to improve.

In a busy day it is easy to see how such things get missed. Brilliant Salespeople make sure these important but not urgent tasks get done. Remember, it is not the activity that counts, it is the result you achieve from your activity.

> *'People can generally make time for what they choose to do; it is not really the time but the will that is lacking.'* – Sir John Lubbock, English banker and statesman

Make time for the right things

The next logical question, once we have identified the things on which we should focus to maximise our results, is how we make the time to do these things. The secret is not to try and release huge chunks of time, because this is simply not realistic. Perhaps the most that we can expect (from re-prioritising the things we focus on at present) is to find another 15–20 minutes per day to spend on the important tasks. If this is going to work, we need to make sure that the goals we set for these tasks are manageable, remembering that anything we do is likely to bring a benefit.

The table opposite sets out some examples of what these goals might be.

Important task	Possible goals
Increase the number of prospects contacted who agree to meet with me	– Monitor my call results so that I have accurate data on my ratio of prospects to meetings (5 minutes) – Ask my manager to listen to my calls and give objective feedback (15 minutes) – Reflect on my calls immediately after making them to identify what worked and what did not work (5 minutes)
Increase the number of prospects whom I can visit in a day	– Create a specific agenda for my meeting so I stay focused and manage the meeting time (10 minutes) – Plan trips further in advance so that I can obtain more prospects to visit in the area (ongoing but no more than 5 minutes a day)
Improve my conversion ratio	– Review the last six months' prospect and sales order numbers so that I know my conversion ratio and set a target ratio based on this (15 minutes) – Focus on coming up with some great open questions to use in needs identification (15 minutes) – Consider the regular objections I get, and amend how I present the product to manage these better (20 minutes x 3 days)

It is easy to come up with the short-term goals that will make the difference and you then simply need to put these tasks in your diary and commit to taking action. You will find that the more you choose to set these manageable goals around important tasks, the more likely you are to achieve them. Over time, this will make a dramatic, positive difference to your performance and results.

brilliant exercise

Make a list of the important but non-urgent tasks that would make a real difference to your performance. Get as specific as you can in terms of what you need to do. Break the tasks down into smaller, short-term goals that you could accomplish in 20 minutes. Prioritise them based on their likely positive impact and put them in your diary. Commit to doing at least one of them this week.

'Things which matter most should never be at the mercy of things which matter least.' – Johann Wolfgang von Goethe, German writer

brilliant recap

How we manage and use our time has a direct and significant impact on our sales performance and results. In this section we have covered the following points:

- Brilliant Salespeople spend time on the right things – they are proactive.
- Make a conscious effort to spend time focusing only on those things over which you have some control or influence. Spending time focusing or worrying about things you cannot control is wasteful and detracts from your results.
- Consider how you prioritise and on what activities you spend your time now. Often these are the things we either enjoy doing or are under pressure to deliver. This is not the same as focusing on important tasks that move your business forward.
- To spend more time on the important, non-urgent, tasks you need first to define what they are.
- Break these important tasks into small goals that will take no more than 20 minutes a day to action.
- Over a period of time, the '20 minutes a day' actions will add up to making a significant positive impact on your sales performance.

One very important but non-urgent aspect of our work as Brilliant Salespeople is planning, and significant benefits come from spending time on it. But how do we get the best from our planning and what is important? Read the next chapter to find out more.

Planning for success

Planning implies coming up with a method, procedure or approach in advance of taking action. Perhaps a good example of the benefits of planning is this quote from the entrepreneur Donald Trump:

'When I started out in business, I spent a great deal of time researching every detail that might be pertinent to the deal I was interested in making. I still do the same today. People often comment on how quickly I operate, but the reason I can move quickly is that I've done the background work first, which no one usually sees. I prepare myself thoroughly, and then when it is time to move ahead, I am ready to sprint.'

Planning is another one of those things we know that we should do and convince ourselves we are doing well enough. The Brilliant Salesperson plans for actions rather than results and makes plans around the important things. In sales, a lot of 'plans' are actually targets. We might have a sales plan that relates to a revenue or margin figure, for example. We need to plan the aspects of our sales work so that we can achieve the results that we want. Almost every aspect of what we do could benefit from a plan. The major benefit of planning is that we can be more objective and thoughtful about what we need to do to achieve our goals and ensure that we do not miss out important aspects that could make a difference.

almost every aspect of what we do could benefit from a plan

> *'Planning is bringing the future into the present so that you can do something about it now.'* – Alan Lakein, US author on personal time-management

Let us look at some specific things we can plan and what we should take account of when we are planning. These are examples rather than a definitive list.

Planning prospecting activities

We can plan a number of aspects of our prospecting activity, as suggested in this table:

The time needed to prospect	By taking the sales target and dividing it by the average order value you can arrive at the number of sales you need to make. By using current conversion rates, you can come up with a total number of prospects whom you need to contact. You can then factor the time taken to generate a prospect (maybe through your own prospecting activity, such as cold calling) to arrive at the amount of time required. This activity can then be planned into your calendar. So, if my average order value is £1,000 and I have a new account sales target for the year of £200,000, then I know I need 200 sales over 12 months to achieve target. If I know that for every 3 prospects I have, I convert 1 into a sale, then I need 200 x 3 prospects to make my sales target. Now I can plan how much time it will take to generate 600 prospects using current or potential prospecting activities.
Our strategy for contact	We might plan how we should best make contact with our prospects. We may have an existing strategy but choose to brainstorm new ideas to get to the same or a different type of purchaser. Based on the outcome of this brainstorming, we can then come up with a detailed plan.

Our key messages	We can plan how best to communicate the benefits and differentiators of our product or service to potential customers. Different types of customer might be interested in different messages.
How to improve conversion rates	Once we know our conversion rates we can make a plan that can help improve them. This might include changing aspects of our sales process and reviewing results, for example.

Planning meetings

Brilliant Salespeople make time to plan their meetings so that they maximise the chance of achieving their objectives from them. This planning often does not take a lot of time but can make a significant difference. We know of lots of salespeople who do not plan in this area – they turn up and 'wing it'. For that small investment in planning they could dramatically improve their outcome.

Prospect meetings	Research the prospect, e.g. using the internet Set an agenda for the meeting Plan your key questions Think about who should be there Plan your own outcomes – what do you want to achieve?
Presenting solutions	Think about what the prospect needs to know Put yourself in the prospect's shoes to bring greater empathy Plan how you will make your points clear and compelling What questions might come up and how will you address them? If presenting with others, who will do what and how will you manage handovers?
Internal sales meetings	Do the necessary preparation Understand what is expected of you in the meeting Think about issues on the agenda so that you can contribute Look at, and action if appropriate, the minutes from the previous meeting

Planning the efficient use of time

Client/prospect visits	Plan your territory and visits so that you maximise efficiency and use of your time Think about the time needed realistically to cover your meeting agenda
Customer contact	Plan how often you need to contact your clients and prospects and schedule this activity
Administration	Take things with you that you can do if you find yourself with a little time before or after a meeting or while you are travelling Plan time to do this aspect of your role

brilliant tip

Visit **www.brilliant-selling.com** for more ideas to inform your planning, or use the templates within the free resource pack (send an email to **resources@brilliant-selling.com** to receive this pack).

Planning tips

'A good plan today is better than a perfect plan tomorrow.' – Anon

We are often planning in a changing environment. We are not likely to have perfect or complete information and we must resist the temptation to get into 'planning paralysis'. Do not let perfect be the enemy of the good. Often we create a plan only to find that it changes as soon as we start implementing it. This is fine. If we did not plan we would have a scattergun approach that would make it very difficult to review what is working and what we need to do differently. Once you have a plan that is good, it is best to implement it rather than try and improve it by another 5 per cent from 85 to 90 per cent perfect.

Remember, you do not need to plan everything; you just need to plan the right things. Also, the best plans are often the simplest – they are easier to monitor. If you get into the habit of planning the important things, such as meeting agendas and thinking about the questions a prospect is likely to ask in a presentation, you will be surprised at how little time it adds and how much of a difference it makes!

> the best plans are often the simplest – they are easier to monitor

'It pays to plan ahead. It wasn't raining when Noah built the ark.' – Anon.

Planning is best done in advance of the activity concerned. If you start to plan too late you are under pressure for a result and your planning will be far less effective. It is also difficult to be objective about a situation if you are planning in the middle of it.

brilliant recap

In this chapter on planning the key points that we covered were:

- A lot of plans are actually targets and what is missing is the thought about 'how' rather than 'what'.
- You should focus on making a good plan – do not get caught up with 'perfect'.
- Often the plans that make the most positive difference take the shortest time to compile. These include meeting agendas, possible questions a prospect might ask and researching the client so that you can add value.
- Planning in advance of an activity makes it easier to be more objective and to review the results afterwards.

Goal setting is an important part of planning. The next chapter looks at how you can ensure you set the right goals to support your success.

Setting the right goals

A while back I was in the market for a new car. I had gone through all the magazines and chosen the manufacturer, model, colour and specification. The next day I was travelling back from a sales call and it struck me how many of this specific colour, model and make of car I was seeing on the roads. The point is that these cars were on the road before I had made my choice. I was seeing these cars but my brain was simply not drawing them to my attention because I had not 'told it' they were of interest to me. Has this ever happened to you? After you set a goal and put your mind on something specific, your brain begins to notice those things that relate to the goal and your achievement of it. Bizarrely, my co-author Jeremy cannot visit any new town without automatically spotting hairdressing salons, as he used to work for L'Oréal!

Brilliant Salespeople set goals for themselves

'Without goals, and plans to reach them, you are like a ship that has set sail with no destination.' – Fitzhugh Dodson, US clinical psychologist

Goal setting is critical in sales. We are often given sales goals in the form of targets but Brilliant Salespeople set goals for themselves. Goals come in many shapes and sizes and they can and should be set for any activity where you want to achieve a specific result. Goals focus our attention and tell our brain what is important to us so that it notices things that support their achievement.

Goals that get results

There are a few golden rules for setting brilliant goals and it is worth checking any goal that you set yourself against the following criteria:

- Is the goal in your control?
- Is the goal SMART?
- Does it motivate you?

Is the goal in your control?

Make sure that any goal is set around something of which you are in control. For example, if the outcome that you want is to be the top salesperson in your company or to be promoted to sales manager within a year, focus on the element of this outcome that you can control and set goals around it.

goals we set have to be things we can control ourselves

brilliant example

Desired outcome	To be the top salesperson in the team
What can I not control?	The sales figures of the other salespeople
What can I control?	My own performance relative to the amount of prospecting activity I do, the conversion rates I achieve and the average order value
Possible goals	To spend a minimum of three hours each week between the hours of 8am and 9:30am on prospecting telephone calls
	To achieve a conversion rate from 'prospect' to 'qualified lead' of 3:1
	To achieve an average order value of x or higher

Aspirational outcomes are important – they give us inspiration and motivation – but the goals we set have to be things we can control ourselves, which will take us towards the desired outcome.

Is the goal SMART?

SMART is an acronym for:

Specific: What do I want? In which situations? With which people? Make the goal as specific as you can. For example, 'I want to be successful' is not specific, whereas 'I want to achieve a client base of 40 customers in the local government sector with an average order value of x' is.

Measurable: How, specifically, will I know when I have achieved it? What are the measures?

Achievable: Is it a realistic goal for me to set? Can I achieve it? Do I need anybody's support or assistance?

Relevant: Is it relevant to my other goals, my aspirations, etc.?

Time-bound: Pick a specific date rather than 'by the middle of next year'. The brain prefers a specific deadline.

Does it motivate you?

This might sound strange but not all goals motivate us. Sometimes we set a goal that is either so big or so far in the future that it does not seem 'real' enough to motivate us. It might be inspirational but sometimes we need to focus on goals where it is easier to see how we can achieve them. Make sure that you set interim milestones for those big, long-term goals.

For example, if you want your product to be the market leader in a particular sector within a three-year timeframe, you might set milestones of the number and type of customer in the next 12 months, a minimum number of customer testimonials in year two, and so on. By setting smaller goals along the way to achieving the big one, you can celebrate success, make sure you are on track and stay motivated.

What should we set goals for in our selling?

There are two main areas of our sales work where goals make real sense:

- Our individual performance.
- What we want from specific situations.

Individual performance

Break your sales performance down and set specific goals for the aspects that you most want to develop or that will make the biggest positive difference. These might include:

- The amount of time I spend in prospecting activity.
- The conversion rate I achieve at each stage of the sales process.
- My sales revenue achievement.
- The number and quality of open questions I ask in order to identify needs.
- The number of customers I talk to each week.
- The number of times that I ask for, and receive, referrals from existing customers.
- The number of board-level contacts I make in each of my customers.

Specific situations

Think about specific sales situations you approach, or are faced with, and set goals for them. These might include:

- What I want to achieve from this sales meeting with my prospect.
- What I want to gain from visiting this networking event.
- What I want to find out from my research on this prospect.
- What I want to learn from attending this training course specifically.
- What I want to get done by the end of today.

brilliant tip

Visit **www.brilliant-selling.com** for more ideas on goal setting and use the templates in the free resource pack (send an email to **resources@brilliant-selling.com** to receive this pack).

'Think little goals and expect little achievements. Think big goals and win big success.' – Abraham Lincoln, 16th US President

Brilliant Salespeople make goal setting a habit: each year, each month, each week, each day and each meeting.

brilliant recap

If we set effective goals in sales we are more likely to achieve the results that we want:

- Setting goals enables the brain to notice things that take you towards what you want to achieve.
- Brilliant Salespeople set goals around their performance and specific situations, such as meetings and what they want to achieve each day.

- Focus on setting goals around those things that you can control or influence.
- Break big goals down into smaller milestone goals to make them more motivating.
- Make sure goals are specific, measurable, achievable, relevant and time-bound.

Goals can be set for many aspects of our selling. One thing that should inform our goal setting is the sales information to which we have access, and this is covered in the next chapter.

Managing sales information

It may not be too much of a stretch to say that most salespeople did not get into selling to analyse data. While selling has a lot to do with human interaction, there is however, an important role for data and for spending time understanding it, interpreting it and using it to improve our performance and results.

Data can often be an objective window into why we are achieving a certain result and a clue as to what to do about it. Without data you are not fully in control of your selling and may well only start to notice a potential problem when it is too late!

> *'The person who knows HOW will always have a job. The person who knows WHY will always be his boss.'* – Diane Ravitch, US education historian

What data should you pay attention to in sales?

This will vary depending on what you are selling, how you are selling and to whom you are selling, but there are some categories that are worth focusing on here. Data and information about:

- what your market is doing. This might include trends, key issues, changes in how they do business, etc.
- what specific prospects/customers are doing. How are they doing compared to their competition, what are their current issues, what does the annual report say, what is their

revenue/margin with you this year compared to the last three years, etc.?

- how other salespeople are doing within the company. What are their revenues, margins, pipeline figures, etc.?
- how you are doing. Comparisons year on year, quarter on quarter around the important metrics against which your performance is judged.

How should you use it?

The first rule is to make sure you are objective about what the data are telling you. It is easy for us to read things into data that are based on our assumptions or what we want to believe. One great use for data is to help us form questions and hypotheses that we can then find ways to test. In testing these ideas we get more information upon which to base our sales decisions.

make sure you are objective about what the data are telling you

Be sure to keep interpretation of data objective and relevant!

For example, if monthly sales data is showing that our average order value on a certain product is x and that this is 12 per cent lower than half of our colleagues, we might do a number of things:

- Work out what a 12 per cent increase would mean against the number of orders for that product that we close in a month, in terms of increased revenues. This might give us the motivation to work on improving the figure.
- Look perhaps at sales data across all products for our colleagues, to see if there are any patterns; maybe other products with which they seem successful. This will give us a wider perspective for the data.
- Plan actions such as talking to colleagues about what they are doing relative to selling this particular product.

Sales pipeline data

The best salespeople manage their sales cycle – their pipeline. This pipeline management enables them to know more objectively if the relative activities and numbers in each stage of the pipeline are enough to achieve the result they need, while also eliminating peaks and troughs in sales, so that they can plan accordingly. They are disciplined and balanced in how and where they apply their time and effort.

the best salespeople manage their sales cycle – their pipeline

A lot of companies have some form of system (either manual or based on a software application) that manages data on the sales pipeline. This can be very useful if used correctly. You might have access to data about the number of prospects at each stage of the sales cycle, which can give you conversion rate information. You can use this by evaluating each step of the process and your performance, to get ideas as to where an improvement would make the most positive difference. Or you might be able to get empirical data about the number of prospects at each stage of your pipeline together with potential deal size, in order to help plan your activity and become aware of specific areas that you need to address.

Sales pipeline information differs dramatically, but Brilliant Salespeople take the time to understand what the data is telling them and use it to inform their sales activities.

A pipeline often enables you to track the following information:

- **Individual prospects**: their name, the size of the deal, where they are in the cycle and the date it is likely to close.
- **Sales forecast**: maybe by week, month or quarter in terms of revenue or margin.
- **Each stage of the sales cycle**: showing the number of prospects at each stage and the value of possible deals at each stage.
- **A percentage probability of the sale happening**: to give a better idea of what the actual figures are likely to be. Sometimes this 'closing probability' is linked to each stage of the cycle. For example, if you are still qualifying the opportunity it may have a 20 per cent probability, whereas if you are presenting the solution it might be a 60 per cent probability.

brilliant tip

Email **resources@brilliant-selling.com** to receive a free resource pack with examples of sales pipeline forms.

brilliant recap

Sales information can be a real help in achieving results.

- We need to make time to look at the data – this brings objectivity to our planning and where we spend our time.
- Sales pipeline data is a strategic planning tool – and can help ensure that we achieve consistency to avoid 'feast or famine' results.
- We can use pipeline data to work out conversion rates and decide which of the activities in which we engage need more attention or development.
- Used correctly, sales information helps us to avoid nasty surprises!

Managing sales information effectively requires logic and objective analysis, but we then need to be able to utilise this with a prospect – and that means we need to influence. Part 3 of this book focuses on your power to influence.

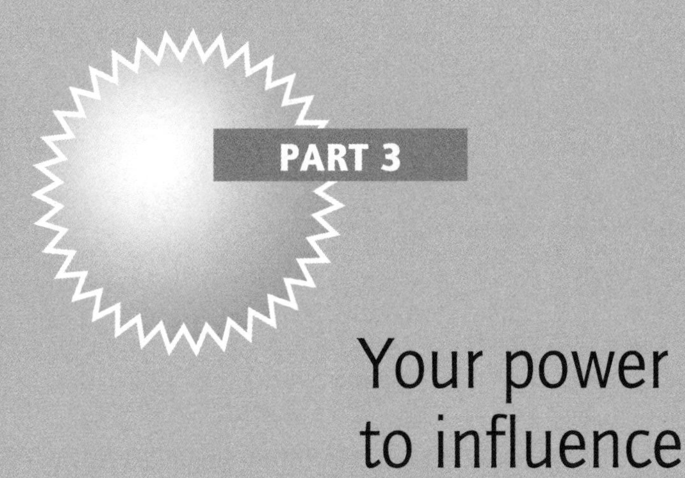

Your power to influence

I enjoy sport, and many years ago I was looking forward to playing in an Easter hockey festival. A few days before the weekend I started getting pains in my stomach. The pain worsened and I ended up in hospital with appendicitis. After the operation, and during the recovery phase, I got to know a fellow patient, Stanley Burns. He shared my passion for books and we became friends. One day in the hospital he was telling me about a time in his life when he traded jade in 1930s China. His story included an adventure with Somerset Maugham when he had appendicitis on the Yangtze River! I asked him: 'How were you, a Plymouth lad in your twenties and not well travelled, able to sell jade in China?' I remember his answer well – he said, 'It was simple really. At first I was no good at all and then I started thinking like a Chinese person – as soon as I started doing this, I began to be successful'.

We have all heard of the expression 'Put yourself in the other person's shoes'. If you have a good sense of what the other wants, can think like the person you want to influence, behave like and respect the person, then your chances of sales success increase dramatically. The core question is – how do you do that?

In this section, we are concerned with ethical influencing in sales situations. The key here is your objective – if you are trying to manipulate for a quick gain you can, potentially, use many unethical behaviours. However, if you believe there is a match between your service/product and what a customer wants, then of course you want to influence and close the deal. The reality is that you are always influencing, whether you like it or not. The central questions are – do you know what effect you are having, and are you making conscious choices about how you are influencing your prospects and customers?

There are some fundamentals that have to be in place if we want to get people to buy from us – whatever sales scenario or market we operate in. This section will cover some of these fundamentals and provide you with key information, which will allow you to influence people easily, both in your professional and personal lives.

Here are some questions at the heart of this influencing section that will be addressed:

- What needs to be in place to become a KPI (Key Person of Influence – see Chapter 3)?
- How do we influence the modern buyer?
- What are the key elements that will allow someone to be influenced effortlessly?
- How do we consistently get into a positive state to influence well?
- What sort of questions will make the biggest difference?
- How can we demonstrate that we are actively paying attention to a buyer?
- How do we negotiate effectively and get an agreement that works?

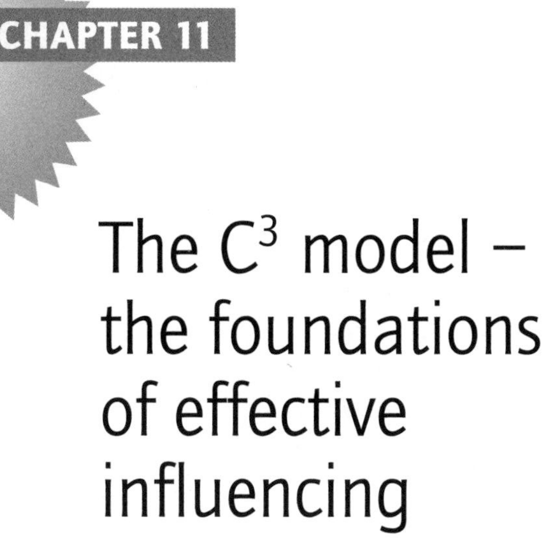

CHAPTER 11

The C^3 model – the foundations of effective influencing

Influencing is about producing an effect on an individual or group by imperceptible or intangible means. It is about shaping and determining a response, which will be linked to your outcome. Influencing done well is, of course, closely linked to persuasion, which is the process of changing attitudes, beliefs and opinions.

We often think of influencing in a negative sense and have a rather sensible approach in the UK: buyer beware. The reality is that we are influenced at a conscious and unconscious level all the time – through the people with whom we interact and, of course, via marketing and advertising. Do you really think you are making completely conscious buying decisions when you are in the supermarket?

we are influenced at a conscious and unconscious level all the time

'Influence may be the highest level of human skills.' – Anon.

Just consider this for a moment – think of a time in the last six months when you wanted to buy something. You did not need to be persuaded about a product, the price was acceptable and you walked into a store but left without buying the product. If this has ever happened to you, there is a good chance that the person serving influenced you *not* to buy! The salesperson may have done one (or more) of the following:

- Confused you with feature overload.
- Did not listen to what you wanted.
- Ignored you.
- Did not ask you any questions.
- Asked you what you perceived as an annoying question.
- Did not have the exact information you wanted.
- Seemed to lack confidence.

Evidence suggests that, when confronted with these sorts of scenarios, many people are prepared to pay more for exactly the same service or product from another supplier or online.

Maybe you have also had the experience where you bought something from someone you really liked and then suffered from buyer's remorse at some stage after the sale had taken place, as you realised you did not really need what you had bought.

The C^3 model

What is going on here? How is it that even sophisticated people are influenced in this way? It seems, on the face of it, entirely irrational. Well, what is happening is that you are being affected by the foundations of influencing – confidence, credibility and connection. What we call the C^3 Model of Influence.

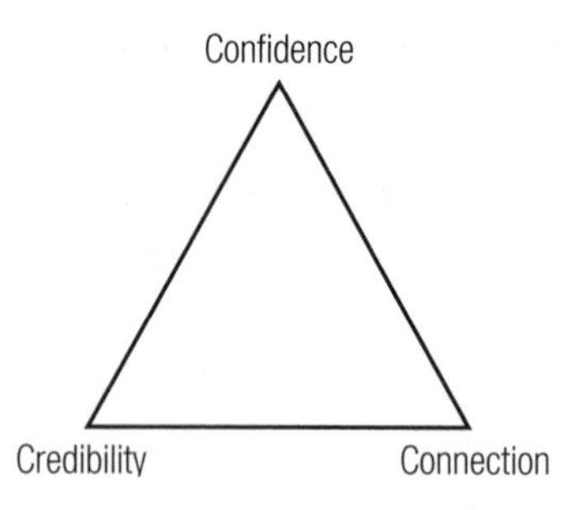

In most sales situations it is unlikely that anyone will buy anything from a salesperson unless they have demonstrated **confidence**, established **credibility** and built a **connection** with you. In many of your own sales scenarios you already achieve this – otherwise you are unlikely to motivate people to buy. But do you know how to do this consciously and at will? What can you do to be confident, ooze credibility and build a connection that allows someone to buy effortlessly? Here is how …

How to be confident

I wonder if you have ever had this sort of experience – a day or part of a day when everything went right in your sales job. People said yes, there was an ease in the way you dealt with any problems and you got a huge kick out of all your interactions. You may have experienced what positive psychologist Mihály Csíkszentmihályi calls a 'flow state', either in a sales role or another job or activity. This is a mental state of operation in which you are fully involved in an experience. We have other terms for this – 'in the zone', 'on the ball', 'really with it' – a time when there is focus and absorption in the task, a balance between ability level and challenge in an activity, which is intrinsically rewarding. This sort of positive state or a lighter version of this state is a great way to be when we are selling or influencing others. But do you have any idea how to access this state at will?

> *'Even when I was in the orphanage, when I was roaming the street trying to find enough to eat, even then I thought of myself as the greatest actor in the world. I had to feel the exuberance that comes from utter confidence in yourself. Without it, you go down to defeat.'* – Charlie Chaplin, English actor and film director

So you need to be in a confident state when you sell. If not, your lack of confidence will leak out of you through your unassertive body language, weak voice or unconvincing language.

The state you are in will affect everything else going on in you and around you. But, what exactly is a state?

brilliant definition

A **state** is the way you are feeling at a given moment – a combination of thought, emotion and physiology. It combines our mental pictures, sounds, feelings, physical energy and breathing.

We often think of a state in a negative way, as in 'he's in a right state' or 'she's got out of bed the wrong side today'. We go through many different states in any single day. You may, at times, be happy, sad, depressed, nervous, excited or energised.

Nowadays, many top sports people use sports psychologists to help train them mentally to win. It is part of their routine. Why? Because it works! Accessing the right state is critical to being at your best when you sell. When you are feeling really good about yourself, and confident, you will sell well. Things going on inside us affect the success of any sales performance. The state we are in impacts on our physiology, affecting our behaviour – which is what your client or prospect will see when you are selling. State management is the ability to choose the most appropriate state at any given moment. So, take a moment to define how to do this easily …

brilliant exercise

What sort of state do you want to be in when you sell?

Decide the state you would ideally like to be in when you sell to both prospects and existing customers. What name would you give to this state?

How do I get into this resourceful selling state?

So you now know your ideal selling state – confident, relaxed, focused, or whatever you have chosen. Can you get into this state at will? Are you secretary of your own state? Or do you allow others to affect your state?

brilliant exercise

Here are the steps to get into a resourceful state:

1. Recall a time when you were in your desired state.
2. Either look up towards your left or close your eyes, and go back into that time now and remember what you saw, heard and felt – make sure you see a picture, through your own eyes, that is a movie in full colour, and that you can see the picture easily.
3. Now notice how it makes you feel in the present. Many people start feeling the state. When this happens, know that you can repeat this process and access this state whenever you want.

Here are some additional ideas about accessing a state that will allow you to sell at peak performance:

- Get physiologically comfortable – get balanced.
- Get your breathing under control – five deep breaths held for five seconds will usually do it, deep into your diaphragm.
- Look up to the right, relax and expand your awareness to your peripheral vision. Allow yourself just to relax. This is much better than looking down, which can increase anxiety or get you thinking too much!

Being in a resourceful state leads inexorably to what most of us think of as a positive attitude. Our Brilliant Selling survey (**www.brilliant-selling.com**) reveals that top salespeople understand the importance of attitude in selling. Indeed, asked

> top salespeople understand the importance of attitude in selling

to choose whether attitude or skill was more important, 77 per cent said attitude. This positive attitude is also likely to be there for you if you decide on a successful outcome for every major meeting. What will good look like? Imagine what it will be like to progress or take the order. What would you see, hear and feel? I remember when I was working for a big corporate and they offered a new Mini car as a first prize for a new product launch. I immediately imagined myself winning the car and walking up to collect the key on stage. Partly because I created such a vivid picture in my mind, I literally drove myself to succeed and it was quite a feeling when I strode up and took possession of the vehicle.

Establish credibility

Credibility derives from the Latin 'credo', which means 'I believe'. You need to be believable to sell. Indeed, buyers are sorting for this when they meet you. What does this mean in practice? Here are ten top tips to establish credibility when selling:

1. **Acquire as much knowledge as possible**: of the customer, product/service, market and competition.
2. **Add value – all the time!** At every meeting. Before any meeting ask yourself, what can I tell them that they do not already know? Think about how websites work well – there is often a huge amount of content given away free, which will work on establishing loyalty from the user.
3. **Prepare effectively**: set the agenda, define an outcome, do the research, think what questions the buyer is going to ask.
4. **Execute efficiently**: do what you say you are going to do. Under-promise and over-deliver, keep your word, be consistent, follow through and make clear agreements that are measurable.

5. **Establish multiple links into the organisation**: get an organisational chart, network, meet people and get yourself known.
6. **Avoid 'selling' too early**: ask questions and listen first.
7. **Take responsibility**: we once worked with an organisation where there was a 'they' culture, as in 'they' were the internal people who did not support the sales team sufficiently well. You *are* your company, so speak about 'us' and 'we' and take responsibility for mistakes.
8. **Present with enthusiasm**: whether it is formally or informally, present sales materials with passion.
9. **Make your buyers feel special**. Do you know why people stop buying? The reasons are:
   - 1 per cent die.
   - 3 per cent move away.
   - 5 per cent follow a friend's or relative's recommendation.
   - 9 per cent find an alternative they perceive to be better quality or value.
   - 14 per cent are dissatisfied with the product/service.
   - And a massive 68 per cent of people leave a business because of … indifference. They take their business elsewhere simply because they do not feel valued.
10. **Have the courage to say no**: they will respect you. Salespeople often say yes when they mean no and then have to backtrack!

Build a connection

'Paul is the most generous man with whom I've ever worked. We had a fantastic ***rapport*** *shooting* Butch Cassidy. *It was one of the happiest experiences of my life.'* – Robert Redford, US actor (1972 comment on Paul Newman)

Credibility comes first in selling, followed closely by connection/rapport (the two words are interchangeable).

brilliant definition

Rapport is a harmonious **connection** with another person, which often takes place outside conscious awareness.

> credibility comes first in selling, followed closely by connection

It is about connectivity, getting on the same wavelength. Connection, or rapport, is the naturally occurring dance that happens when people meet. Sometimes rapport occurs spontaneously. However, there are specific skills you can learn that enhance rapport and increase your effectiveness as a communicator and salesperson in business situations.

We have a natural connection with friends and family. In selling, rapport is the ability to relate to others in a way that creates a climate of trust and understanding. People generally do not buy from people they do not like.

brilliant exercise

Think of a recent face-to-face purchase when you bought something; now think about a time when you did not buy. What are the distinctions in terms of connection? What do you notice?

Connection when I bought	Connection when I did not buy

People have a tough time trusting salespeople with their time, money and business. Many people will not even want to talk to you. Welcome to reality! Your customers and prospects are busy and may feel that speaking with you is a waste of time. Many of your prospects may not even see a need for your product, or may be content with the version they already have. So, if you decide connection is a good thing, you will have to build it quickly.

It could be argued that the connection element has been over-played in sales training over the years, especially with the use of NLP (Neuro-Linguistic Programming), so that most salespeople understand its importance in the sales process. However, establishing and building rapport is a simple first step to showing you are genuinely interested, and can act as a bridge to a mutually beneficial relationship. It depends on what you do, say and notice. Sometimes we meet people we do not like, but in selling if they do not warm to you they will start putting up barriers and the bridge can become a drawbridge!

brilliant tips

Here are ten top tips to establish and build connection:

1 **Lobby in advance**: telephone and email someone so you build the connection early.

2 **Do the chit-chat**: generally speaking, we tend not to dive straight into the business conversation. I was once training some business people from Brazil and they were telling me that it is thought rude in their country if you do not do what we describe as 'small talk' in the UK for at least 45 minutes! Avoid 'So, how's business?' – it might be terrible right now and get you off on the wrong footing.

3 **Share personal information**: find out more about their other interests and what makes them tick. People are 1,000 times more interested in themselves than they are in you (or your product or service). When you have discovered things – holiday destinations, birthday, hobbies etc. – remember and use the details.

4 **Be like them**: people buy from people who are like themselves. Identify how they move and speak and then copy them subtly. This idea is called matching and mirroring – see opposite for more information.

5 **Listen, listen, listen**: and then listen some more.

6 **Ask questions**: it shows you are interested and following the thoughts of the buyer.

7 **Look as though you are interested**: demonstrate curiosity through attentive body language, e.g. smile, nod or grunt!

8 **Be friendly**: I was in an audience recently and was amazed at the easy and straightforward way that the speaker lost his audience by being deliberately provocative and unfriendly.

9 **Lighten up and laugh**: Nothing is more powerful than humour when it comes to building rapport quickly. Laughter is the spark that can ignite interest and cordiality between you and the person you are influencing; it is hard to laugh with a person and not feel comfortable around them. Some salespeople take their job far too seriously! So, lighten up! If you make them laugh, they may just buy!

10 **Finally – get to the point!** State your objective and why they should listen. Avoid clichéd and insincere reasons such as saving money, increasing productivity and other transparent and ineffective reasons they have heard from many salespeople before you. Prospects and buyers do not enjoy having their time wasted by salespeople playing games.

For those of you who have not heard of matching and mirroring, here is a quick explanation.

Match and mirror

We were approached a couple of years ago by a health company focusing on NHS trusts. It so happened that the CEO called us on the telephone in our office. They had found one of our business, RTP (**www.rtpc.co.uk**), on the web. This is usually pot luck and means he will have called a number of other businesses. The CEO was worried about some disharmony on the board and was looking to do some teamwork training for this group. I asked what he was looking for from a consultancy and he used the word 'rigorous' quite a few times. I called Tom and suggested he take the opportunity. Sure enough, when he spoke to the guy, the same word was used. We decided to include the word five times in the proposal. Well, we won the work and I sent an email asking for the reason he had chosen us. I still have his response – 'We felt you had a very *rigorous* approach to helping us develop the board'. Now of course there were other factors, but we certainly spoke his language!

Matching and mirroring is a tool introduced to the world by Richard Bandler and John Grinder of NLP fame (Neuro-Linguistic Programming). They modelled Milton Erickson, a leading psychotherapist in the USA, and noticed that Erickson was outstanding at building rapport with his patients. Rapport building, or establishing a connection in our C^3 model, is based around the idea of pacing the person you are attempting to influence. Pacing is about putting yourself in the shoes of the other person, seeing the situation from where the other party is sitting:

- Why are they raising the issues they are?
- What constraints do they have?
- What pressures are they under?
- How do they think?
- What do they want?

Rapport is a way of demonstrating that you are like the other party. People tend to buy from people who are like them. As a rule we prefer to say yes to the requests of people we know and like. The liking rule produces assent. So, if you match and mirror you will seem to be similar. The art is to do it in a subtle way – copying some aspect of their behaviour, which, done well, can bring about the 'harmonious connection'. Done badly or incongruously, of course, it can be annoying! So if the buyer has an unusual physical tic, please do not match this!

You can match another person using all three of the communication channels when you sell – the visual, the verbal and the voice. This is how you do it:

Communication channel	What you can match
The visual (body language)	Posture
	Gestures
	Breathing
	Energy level
	Facial expressions
The verbal (what they say)	Specific language patterns (e.g. 'rigorous')
	Beliefs (see Part 1)
	Values (see Part 1)
	Humour
	Common interests
The voice (how they say what they say)	Tonality
	Rhythm
	Speed
	Volume

brilliant example

Often when you get on an aeroplane the first person you will hear is the captain, as in 'Welcome aboard. My name is Captain Cassell ...'. At some point you will also hear the flight attendant. Next time you are on a plane, listen carefully to the way they speak. You may well notice these differences in their voices:

Captain – vocal qualities	Flight attendant – vocal qualities
Slow	Fast
Intonation goes down at the end of the sentence or phrase	Intonation goes up at the end of the sentence or phrase
Uses pauses	Uses few pauses
Short, clipped sentences	Long, possibly rambling sentences
Monosyllabic	Lots of variety and musicality in the voice

Essentially the captain uses a 'credible' voice pattern, while the flight attendant uses a 'rapport' voice. Think Barack Obama or David Cameron for credible voice and Stephen Fry or Dawn French for rapport voice. Use both voice patterns when you are trying to influence, and focus on the credible voice pattern when you discuss your service/product and when you want the other person to make a decision. For more information send an email to **resources@brilliant-selling.com**.

You always have the choice of matching or mismatching the other person. There are times when you need to break rapport. If someone is making a decision in a buying situation it may be appropriate, momentarily, to mismatch (the opposite of matching) him so he is making the decision himself.

brilliant recap

If you can first understand the C^3 Model of Influence and then start applying it in all sales situations, you will soon discover its power. You will become like a magnet. In this chapter the key areas that have been covered are:

- Influencing is about producing an effect on an individual or group by imperceptible or intangible means.
- The C^3 Model of Influence is the foundation of effective influencing and if used well can help you to become a KPI (Key Person of Influence).
- Accessing the right state is critical to being at your best when you sell.
- You can become secretary of your own state.
- In our Brilliant Selling survey 77 per cent said that attitude was more important than skill.
- You can become confident by thinking of a time when you were confident, breathing deeply and looking up to the right, rather than looking down.

- Credibility is built around knowledge (of your organisation, your customers' business and the market), preparation and execution.
- It is tough to be influenced by someone you do not like on some level – so find ways to ensure you are liked.
- Matching the customer is a simple and effective way of getting on the same wavelength and tuning in to the way that another is communicating.
- You can use the voice in different ways to establish credibility and build rapport.

A key aspect of effective influence once we have established, credibility and connection and are in the right confident state is our ability to ask the right questions. We can too easily take our questioning skills for granted. The next chapter will help you think about the right questions to ask.

Asking the right questions

When I was learning to be a coach my trainer told me that 'questions are the answer'. It is much the same with selling. You cannot sell well without gathering information and it is tough to gather information without asking questions. Yet, according to a study by the Sales Career Training Institute, salespeople typically spend too much time pitching and not enough time asking the right questions so that they can discover the prospect's/buyer's real concerns and issues, as well as the hot buttons they need to press to get someone to buy.

> *'Judge others by their questions rather than by their answers.'* – Voltaire, French writer and philosopher

So, what are the benefits of asking the right questions?

- By asking the right questions you will demonstrate that you are interested, rather than being focused on making a sale. This will increase the likelihood that the prospect/buyer will open up and that rapport will start to build.
- You will identify what really matters and what the core issues are that you can help to address.
- It gives you an element of control.
- It creates momentum, which is one of the core goals of every sales conversation.
- Questions encourage emotional involvement.

Asking the right questions

Here are seven core principles that will guide you to ask the right questions:

1 Start with an attitude of curiosity

Any salesperson used to a consultative approach will use questions naturally. Asking intelligent questions comes from an attitude of curiosity. Think about it – you are on a 'quest' for information. Anyone who has kids knows that if they are curious about something they will quite naturally ask questions.

Curiosity is infectious. You will soon find the person you are influencing becomes curious about their own situation!

> *'The important thing is not to stop questioning. Curiosity has its own reason for existing.'* – Albert Einstein, German physicist

2 Have a clear outcome for your questions

Ask yourself: what am I trying to achieve by asking questions? This avoids asking unnecessary or random questions.

3 Let the conversation flow naturally

avoid the clipboard approach

Good questioning techniques do not mean that you become an interrogator. Avoid the clipboard approach.

4 Use both open and closed questions

- Open questions start with who, why, what, how, where and when.
- Closed questions elicit a yes/no answer.

There is no evidence that we have ever seen that open questions are more successful in making a sale. However, it is likely that you will start with **open** questions to elicit information and there will be more open questions in a typical sales conversation. Use **closed** questions for clarification and agreement.

5 Make your questions understandable

I have heard many a sales question that is frankly unintelligible. Sometimes people use multiple questions, or ask a question and then answer it themselves, or ask a question that has no real link to what is being discussed. Make sales questions straightforward to understand – often the simple questions are the most powerful. Such as:

often the simple questions are the most powerful

- What do you want?
- What are your key priorities?
- What is really going to make the difference?
- What is working for you?

6 Ask questions that help you pinpoint the dominant buying motivations

Buying motivations and specific needs are not always the same. Buying motivations are about desires and feelings – they are more emotional and intangible.

You can find out what motivates your buyer – what they want – by asking simple questions such as: 'What kind of similar products or services have you bought in the past?'. The knowledge you gain will tell you what benefits to emphasise.

7 Avoid offending your buyers!

Some questions can offend a prospect and cause them to reject you and your ideas.

Avoid leading or 'set up' questions such as, 'You do want your children to have a fair chance, don't you?'. What is the prospect going to say? 'No! It's a tough world – let them sink or swim!'

Nosey, gossipy or overly personal questions can be a real turn-off. Stick to business!

Sometimes your manner can be threatening. Instead of asking, 'How much do you want to spend?', why not phrase it, 'How much had you planned to invest?'.

Focused questions

> *'If you are not moving closer to what you want in sales (or in life), you probably aren't doing enough asking.'* – Jack Canfield, US inspirational self-help author and success coach

So – what areas of questioning are most useful? Research suggests that you will make the most impact if you focus your questioning around these nine areas:

1 Needs and wants

This is absolutely central to the role of the salesperson. Find out more about specific questions that elicit needs and wants by reading the chapter 'Identifying what the prospect wants and needs' in Part 4.

2 Ask the buyer for selection criteria

This is often avoided in sales, so take the initiative and find out who your contact is dealing with right now and who else they might be considering. This will elicit the buyer's criteria and values and will help you align your service/product with what the organisation wants.

The more you can align the values of the buyer with what you can provide in terms of service and delivery, the more you are likely to build a long-term relationship. I had a colleague once who was even more upfront. He used to ask: 'What can I do to win your business?'.

'Selling' is closely linked in meaning to 'serving'. The founder of a client of ours, Sodexo, based his whole strategy on the maxim 'True dignity lies in being of service to others'. How can you be 'of service to others' unless you know how they like to be served?

Here are some questions you might consider:

- What's important in your commercial relationships with suppliers?
- How do you choose your current suppliers?
- How do you decide with whom to do business?
- What do you really value in a salesperson?

---

brilliant exercise

Think about your own selling context. What other questions are there that would work well for you?

---

3 Options

Discover what options your buyer is considering. If they are still at the options stage you can influence their decision making.

Here are some questions you might consider:

- What sort of options are you looking for?
- Who are we up against?
- Who else will you be speaking with in regard to this decision?
- What have you been considering?

---

brilliant exercise

Think about your own selling context. What other questions are there that would work well for you?

---

4 Your service/product

You need to gauge the reaction to your service/product to find out if the buyer is likely to buy and what more information they need to make a decision.

Here are some questions you might consider:

- What are your expectations/requirements for this product/service?
- Have you seen anything else on the market that you especially do not like?
- What further information do you need right now?
- If you do decide to go ahead, what sort of consequences will this have?

---

brilliant exercise

Think about your own selling context. What other questions are there that would work well for you?

---

5 People

Often a buying decision for an organisation will have implications for many people. We sell training, coaching and consultancy services at Brilliant Selling (**www.brilliant-selling.com**), and the people who could be implicated by any decision to use us include sales, HR, operations, marketing, senior management and the board.

Here are some questions you might consider:

- Who will be involved if we progress to the next stage?
- How will people's roles change if you decide to take this product/service?
- Who will be involved in the roll-out?
- What obstacles might be in the way of moving this forward?

brilliant exercise

Think about your own selling context. What other questions are there that would work well for you?

6 Decision making

I remember that I once had three meetings with someone and focused quite a lot of time and energy on the opportunity, before finding out that this person was not the decision maker. Have you ever done something similar? Find out what the decision-making process is and who is involved. This will allow you to focus your energy.

Here are some questions you might consider:

- What can you tell me about your decision-making process?
- Who is the key decision maker within the business?

- How can we help support you internally?
- How much support does this have at the executive level?

brilliant exercise

Think about your own selling context. What other questions are there that would work well for you?

7 Budget

There may or may not be a budget for your offering. It is really helpful to know what amount has been budgeted and with what timescale. When qualifying, assess where a prospect is in their buying cycle. So many salespeople ignore the customer buying cycle and just enforce a rigid sales cycle and wonder why they fail. If a customer has budget available and is ready to buy immediately, then don't ask unnecessary questions. Just close the deal.

We were able once to do a deal with an organisation (later to become a key account) in which they used their budget for the following year and we invoiced them at a later date. They appreciated our flexibility!

Here are some questions you might consider:

- How do you handle budget considerations?
- What price range are you considering?
- Who is paying for this?
- How will the funding for the project be justified?

brilliant exercise

Think about your own selling context. What other questions are there that would work well for you?

8 Momentum/qualifying

Salespeople sometimes spend too long talking to prospects when there is little hope of the prospect buying and where there is no momentum. Ask qualifying questions to establish whether this opportunity is worth pursuing.

Here are some questions you might consider:

- What do you see as the next action steps?
- What is your timeline for implementing/purchasing this type of service/product?
- What constraints do you have in this area?
- What further information do we need to discuss before we move this forward?

brilliant exercise

Think about your own selling context. What other questions are there that would work well for you?

9 Extending the relationship

Of course, questions do not stop when the prospect becomes a customer. Keep on asking questions. If they are delighted by you and your service then ask questions that will allow you to extend the relationship or cross-sell. Or ask them to give you a referral – people will happily do this if they like the product/service and like you! Ask for referrals at the height of the gratitude curve – when they think you are great and have offered an outstanding service, or when they are experiencing the benefits of your product.

> ask for referrals at the height of the gratitude curve

Here are some questions you might consider:

- What else are you looking to address in the business right now, or in the future?
- What other opportunities are there within the business?
- Would it be helpful for you to know what else we offer?
- Who else do you know in business who might like what we have to offer?

brilliant exercise

Think about your own selling context. What other questions are there that would work well for you?

brilliant recap

So, it is not just about asking random questions in order to tease out answers. Brilliant Selling needs to be focused on asking the right questions at the right time to the right person. Successful salespeople use similar skills in this area to a top business coach – they ask questions that:

- are understandable and logical;
- work to help the buyer get clarity;
- and build momentum.

Take your time before each sales meeting you have in the future and ask yourself which questions are most appropriate. Notice that questions are the answer to developing a better understanding of the people you want to influence. The key points from this section are:

- There are seven principles – be curious, have an outcome, let the conversation flow, use open and closed questions, make your questions understandable, identify motivations and avoid offending your buyers.

- Ask focused questions to identify needs and wants, selection criteria, options, reaction to your product/service, the people involved, decision making, budget, qualification and how to extend the relationship.

And, of course, questions are only half of it. If you cannot listen well then you will reduce rapport and be unable to take the customer to the next stage ...

Listening and learning

So, honestly, how good are you at listening? It is almost a cliché that listening is a core sales skill, and yet it is surprising how often salespeople are not focused primarily on listening when they sell. Time and again research suggests that those who really listen tend to be more successful in developing long-term relationships (in selling and life in general!).

> *'The reason why God gave us two ears and one mouth is so that we may listen more and talk less.'* – Diogenes, Greek philosopher

---

brilliant exercise

The following list contains some of the common reasons why salespeople end up *not* listening when selling, or giving the impression of not listening. Have you ever caught yourself thinking them, doing them or saying them, while someone has been speaking to you? They are **listening limiters** and will detract from your effectiveness as a salesperson.

What are your dark and guilty secrets? Tick any of these 15 where you must plead guilty. And, come on, be honest with yourself!

( ) Rehearsing what I am going to say about my product/service while the other person is still talking.

( ) Getting impatient for them to finish so I can start talking.

( ) Not being interested in what they are trying to communicate.

▶

( ) Getting bored and thinking about something else (football, cars, children, what you did last night, holidays, what's your specialty?) while they are speaking.

( ) Thinking 'I'm a busy person' – I have got so many other things I could be getting on with.'

( ) Tapping on my computer keyboard when on the telephone to clients or prospects.

( ) Anticipating what they are going to say before they say it.

( ) Dismissing what they are saying as irrelevant to me.

( ) Finishing off other people's sentences, talking over the other person or interrupting.

( ) Thinking that they are making the point far too slowly to keep me interested.

( ) Thinking, 'Who cares what they are concerned about? I have got my own worries to deal with!'

( ) Preferring to talk rather than keep quiet.

( ) Assuming that they do not know what they are talking about before they speak.

( ) Fidgeting and appearing not to be listening.

( ) Focusing on something else in the room and losing focus.

If you have scored six or more, then this chapter is for you!

Brilliant listeners put aside distractions and really listen. If you are curious you will listen, and if you are really focused on the other party and minimise distractions you can listen with rapt attention.

The benefits can be extraordinary. People open up, they indicate how they like to receive information, they confide in you, they speak about the most interesting and important person in their worlds – themselves!

Active listening

Listening should be an active process in selling and if you develop this muscle you will improve your ability to influence others. There are eight elements of active listening:

listening should be an active process in selling

1. **Value the other party**: show concern and demonstrate that you respect their position.
2. **Listen to what is not said**: pay attention to what is missing, beliefs masked as judgements and the tells of body language.
3. **Limit the time you speak**: many people have low attention spans. Salespeople talk too much – so, minimise your chunks of 'sales speak' to about 30 seconds. You may have heard of the 'power of three' before. Three is a magical number and if you limit yourself to three key points you will come across with more credibility.
4. **Avoid thinking about what you are about to say**: you will miss their message. Do not try and manipulate the conversation by asking questions to which you already know the answer.
5. **Listen to the other party's point of view**: they have a unique perception of the world.
6. **Repeat and reflect the other's comments**: this will ensure you heard them correctly. Alternatively, summarise their words.
7. **Take notes**: but avoid transcripts.
8. **Maintain eye contact**: do this whenever possible.

repeat and reflect the other's comments

Because listening is so critical, here is a comparison of what characterises good and bad listeners.

Good listeners	Bad listeners
React non-verbally, with a smile, a nod or a frown as appropriate	Interrupt frequently and jump to conclusions without waiting for the whole message
Ask questions for clarification	Are so busy formulating their replies that they do not listen to the speaker
Re-state or paraphrase some of the speaker's words to show understanding	Let their thoughts take excursions while the other person is speaking
Display empathy by acknowledging feelings	Get distracted by details
Make regular eye contact with the speaker	Stop listening when the subject matter gets difficult
Pay close attention and do not let their minds wander	Only listen for what they like to hear
Use their thought speed to analyse, sort and store material	Let their emotions take over

brilliant recap

Remember the old adage – we have two ears and one mouth, so use them in that proportion when you sell. Listening really can make a huge difference in building relationships, avoiding misunderstandings and ensuring you hear what your buyers want.

Remember:

- Listening well gets people to open up and they confide in you.
- You need to reduce listening limiters and focus your attention.
- Listening is an active process, so demonstrate your interest.

Brilliant listeners can also be brilliant negotiators, so let's continue our influencing journey by identifying how to negotiate and create win–wins with our buyers.

Negotiating collaboratively

Negotiation is not selling. Equally, you do not necessarily have to negotiate when you sell. Selling is about persuading and convincing. Negotiation is about tying up the loose ends.

brilliant definition

Negotiation is a discussion between two or more parties, which starts with a position of non-agreement. It is a process whereby interested parties resolve disputes, agree upon courses of action, bargain for individual or collective advantage and/or attempt to craft outcomes that serve their mutual interests.

The mistake that many salespeople make is that they assume that negotiation is inevitable. I was once buying a second-hand car and liked the look of a particular one advertised locally. I called the seller and he asked me to come around. Now I do not know much about cars but my ears pricked up when I asked him the price. He said, '£10,000, but I am open to negotiation.' He made an elementary error – he gave away that price immediately. Do you think I paid £10,000? No, of course not. What he should have done was to sell me on the car – housed in a garage, regular service history, the fact he had been the only owner, and so on. But he was too worried about the price he wanted to achieve. Unsurprisingly, I was able to negotiate a much better price!

During a recent house boom my friend had a house for sale at £325,000. He had a number of people interested and was called one morning by the estate agent who said 'Mr and Mrs Stevens are really interested in the house. They would like to offer £315,000, although they are prepared to go to the full asking price if necessary'. Can you imagine my friend's response?

Commercially, a salesperson presents a proposal to a customer. The customer may accept every point in the proposal and a contract is signed. In this situation, no negotiation has taken place. However, if the customer does not accept certain aspects of the proposal, there is an initial position of non-agreement. At this point, a negotiation is required to reach an agreement. Equally, there is no point in a purchasing manager negotiating with a supplier until he is certain that the product/service meets his requirements. To take a non-purchasing/selling example, it is unwise for a recruitment manager to negotiate on salary with a potential employee until it is established that the person is right for the job. Negotiation, then, is about agreeing the conditions with another party (or parties) under which you will do business together.

> *'He who has learned to disagree without being disagreeable has discovered the most valuable secret of a diplomat.'* – Robert Estabrook, US editor and foreign correspondent, *Washington Post.*

Most often you will be negotiating at the end of the sales process, once the buyer has decided there is a potential match between what they want and what you can deliver. However, whenever there is a position of non-agreement you may have to negotiate. These scenarios may include speaking to or meeting the ultimate decision maker, or meeting other interested parties in the organisation.

Negotiation principles

If you start applying these five core principles whenever you are involved in a negotiation, you will improve your results:

1 Work to a win-win

'I will work with them on reaching an agreement with which we are all comfortable.' A long-term business relationship can only work on this collaborative basis. Collaborate comes from the Latin **'collaborare'**, which means 'work with'.

In buying and selling terms, the sellers feel that they are receiving appropriate 'revenue' for the service that they are providing; the purchasers feel that they are receiving value.

2 Decide optimum and fallback positions

In any situation we have our ideal outcome, i.e. the best that we can get from an agreement. This is the optimum. However, implicit in any collaborative negotiation is preparedness to look at the variables, and the 'reshaping' of an original proposition. This *may* involve moving from an ideal situation to something less than ideal, but which is still acceptable to you and the other parties. This is the fallback.

The area between two parties' optimum and fallback positions is the negotiation window, the window of opportunity to reach an agreement:

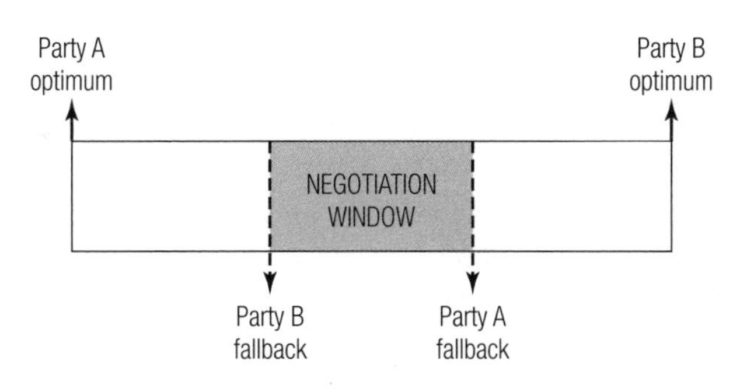

The proposal you put to a customer must be the proposal you believe the customer will buy. It represents your optimum position or just above your optimum.

If you signal: 'This is my proposition but I am prepared to negotiate', it will result in a negotiation!

There is a difference between having calculated your fallback and being prepared to negotiate, if necessary, and *assuming* that you will have to negotiate.

3 Trade concessions

Negotiation often involves conceding – moving from your original position. Fundamental to collaborative sales negotiation is the concept of trading concessions. A lot of salespeople make the mistake of giving away concessions without asking for anything in return.

negotiation often involves conceding

Salespeople have the tendency to cave in when faced with issues around a price or fees. You need to remind yourself of this give-and-take principle: a concession (e.g. reduced price) that involves a cost needs to be balanced by something received that has a value (e.g. extra volume).

Reciprocity is at the heart of what we as humans do, so this principle works well. It permeates much of the exchanges in the sales process. Have you ever had the experience when you were offered a free sample in a supermarket and felt obliged to buy? Robert Cialdini, in his seminal book *Influence*, tells the story of:

> '*... a university professor who tried a little experiment. He sent Christmas cards to a sample of perfect strangers ... the response he received was amazing – holiday cards addressed to him came pouring back from people who had never met nor heard of him.*'
> (Citing a 1976 study by Kunz and Wolcott)

Costs and values are not always in straightforward financial terms. Setting up an exchange process is key to effective negotiation, for example:

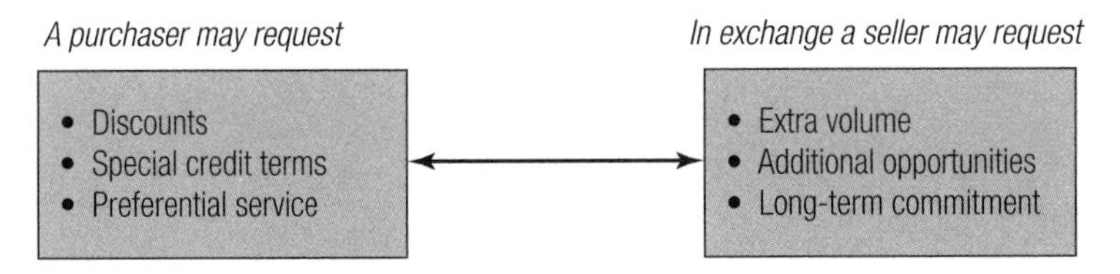

4 Work on all the variables

In selling, there is a danger that price/discount become the focus point in any negotiation. Working on all the variables involves taking a broader view, considering a number of ways to get to an agreement.

> *'Any business arrangement that is not profitable to the other person will in the end prove unprofitable for you. The bargain that yields mutual satisfaction is the only one that is apt to be repeated.'* – B.C. Forbes, Scottish journalist and founder of *Forbes* magazine

An open atmosphere will lead to a positive meeting. Exploring possibilities and generating ideas will assist in building cooperation. The more ideas on the table, the greater the possibilities of an agreement being reached that is acceptable to all parties.

- 'I believe that there are a number of ways to approach this ...'
- 'I have a couple of ideas that may help. Can I ...'
- 'Maybe we could look at ...'
- 'I see two clear ways of providing you with ...'
- 'I think that I can see some solutions ...'
- 'What options are there ...?'

Remember, by suggesting you are not committing – just keeping the discussion open.

5 Avoid assumptions

Salespeople can be guilty of assumptions or mind-reading that bear little relation to what is really happening. Always test assumptions, if you can. Avoid these typical assumptions:

- The same people who were there at the last meeting will be there at the next meeting.
- They are bound to haggle on price.
- All the key people have read the proposal.
- There is nothing for you to offer as a trade.

We were guilty of making assumptions very recently. We walked into a fourth meeting with a prospect, thinking that we might have to negotiate on fees and terms. However, the prospect wheeled out three new big hitters and they spent over an hour grilling us on our proposal. We had to move swiftly back from negotiating to persuading! Fortunately we still won the work, but it reminded us of this important principle.

always test assumptions, if you can

Negotiation tactics

In your everyday life you cannot not negotiate – you do it every day with your family, friends, colleagues and in shops and on the telephone. But what sort of tactics do you use? Are you aware of the ones that really make the difference? Here are seven tactics that you can use in sales negotiations that will sharpen your negotiation skills and allow you to get a better deal for you and your organisation.

1 Build debt

If the other party has negotiated a point that is close to, or at, your fallback position, you may wish to let them know the significance of the concession they have just received.

This can be used at a later stage of the meeting to secure concessions in your favour, or to fend off other demands: 'We can agree to ... in this case, as we can see the benefits of building long-term business with you. I must stress, though, that this payment schedule does represent ...'

Remember, this need not be confrontational.

2 Consistency

People, generally, will act in a consistent way and you can use that to your advantage. For example, appealing for help, when used consciously to relationship-build and/or generate new ideas, is a potentially powerful behaviour. Of course, it depends on a positive relationship having been developed in previous meetings.

3 Use standards and objective criteria

This can help to provide a rationale for a position that is important to you. For example, as a seller:

- A customer may demand 60-day credit terms.
- Your standard terms are 30 days; at the most you could go to 45 days.

Saying to a customer 'Our terms are 30 days' is merely reinforcing the difference in your positions.

However, if you can provide factual data that the industry standard is 30 days and that this is the reason for the position you are taking, it helps show the logic of your case.

4 Summarise

Summarising is a positive behaviour during all stages of a meeting. The longer and more complex the topic, the greater the need to summarise. In the context of negotiation, a summary is important in that it:

- Checks, clarifies and avoids misunderstanding.
- Provides an opportunity, when a sticking point is reached, to emphasise the positive – what has already been achieved. It is therefore a motivator to continue, to reach an agreement: 'I think that this may be a difficult point; however, let's just recap on what we have agreed so far. I believe it will put this point into context ...'.

5 Defer

No matter how well you have planned any face-to-face or telephone meeting the unplanned 'sticking point' can always occur. The danger is that you never move on from that point. Deferring is a technique to move contentious issues to the end of the agenda, enabling other agreements to be made: 'I think that this subject could take us some time ... I suggest that we look at some of the other items first, and come back to this one later. Does that make sense?'.

6 Adjourn

An adjournment can be for ten minutes, two days, or two weeks. Calling for an adjournment provides time to confer with colleagues, speak to your sales manager or carry out calculations, costings and assess implications. This 'breakout' can also help both parties see specific points in perspective. Much better to adjourn than accommodate and then have to backtrack at a later stage: 'We are getting into some detail. I suggest we break for 15 minutes, as I need to contact the office to clarify some specific points.'

7 The flinch

The 'flinch' is a physical or verbal exclamation of surprise/horror at the ridiculous offer/price made by someone in a fee negotiation. Never accept the first offer, and flinch so you demonstrate that the offer is unacceptable. You can flinch big or small, and learn different flinches for different situations. I once worked with a negotiator who was able to summon tears in a heartbeat – a solitary tear rolling down a cheek is one of the more unusual flinches I have come across.

To find out the 30 specific questions you should be asking before you negotiate, email us at **resources@brilliant-selling.com**.

brilliant recap

We have covered a fair amount of material on negotiation here. Let us just recap the key elements of this chapter. We have focused on:

- Treating negotiation as a separate part of the sales process.
- Recognising that negotiating is not inevitable.
- Five key principles: work to a win–win, have an optimum and fallback position, trade concessions, work on variables, avoid assumptions.
- Seven tactics to sharpen your negotiating skills: build debt, consistency, standards and objective criteria, summarise, defer, adjourn, the flinch.

To be truly effective negotiators we need to really understand our buyers and prospects. The next part of the book will help you do this.

PART 4

Understanding buyers and prospects

It was the end of the third quarter. I was a few thousand pounds away from hitting my sales target. I had done well, but not well enough to hit my quarterly target and therefore a retrospective bonus. I surveyed my options – and it was not looking good. So I called some friends – three of my main accounts – and asked them to take an order right now for products they would need in the future. They all obliged and I hit my numbers. The problem? That was almost 20 years ago. In those days, and before then, you could survive in sales by using your native wit and by becoming friends with your customers. Nowadays, however, the sales environment has completely changed and we are met with complex sales scenarios in which we deal with sophisticated, educated, well trained buyers or procurement specialists.

The days of the handshake, the 'do us a favour' approach, are, largely, over. The very ways in which we interact with our clients and prospects are changing. In addition to face-to-face meetings and telephone contact, email has become ubiquitous and video conferencing and virtual meetings are increasing in popularity. We are sometimes faced with ITTs (invitations to tender), panel decisions and specific procurement selection criteria. There is much more rigour in the buying process and expectations have grown enormously about what organisations and buyers want from the salespeople who serve them.

This section considers these questions:

- What are some distinctions in sales approaches?
- Who are the modern buyers?
- What qualities do they want to see from salespeople?
- How do you get in front of buyers?
- How do you identify what the buyers need and want?

CHAPTER 15

How do you sell?

How do you and your organisation sell? What sort of approach do you employ?

Two models of selling

There are essentially two models of selling, and you and your business are likely to adopt the one that best fits your market. Here is a brief overview of the approaches.

Transactional selling

In transactional selling, the focus is on finding prospects with a requirement to develop relationships, focus on features and benefits and to take orders for the desired products or services at an acceptable price to all parties. The customers are likely to have a clear need for a 'standard' product or service and will be interested in sources that can provide it at the right time and at an acceptable price.

in transactional selling, customers are likely to need a 'standard' product or service

Consultative (or solution/relationship) selling

In consultative, solution or relationship selling (all synonyms), the salesperson develops a greater understanding of the challenges faced by the customer and there is likely to be a tailored solution. Questioning and listening become more important than communicating features and positioning statements.

> in consultative selling there is likely to be a tailored solution

The actual purchase decision is often managed through a proposal, contract negotiation and solution delivery. The consultative selling approach is much more common nowadays and is most appropriate for businesses that offer a transformational product or service, such as consulting or specialised, rarely purchased items. Suppliers of transformational products or services find consultative selling necessary, due to the customers' lack of understanding of the possibilities.

> *'Too many salespeople are "talking brochures", trying to show customers how their products or services are better than competitors. Salespeople must become value creators.'* – Neil Rackham English writer and speaker on sales and marketing

Many organisations across the world have trained their sales teams to become business partners and adopt consultative selling strategies. If organisations implement the 'salesperson as business partner' model successfully, there can be huge upsides. The benefits are that:

- It is more difficult for the competition to win business.
- It is possible to access decision makers higher up the food chain.
- Accounts can become more profitable in the long-term.
- There is a higher degree of job satisfaction from salespeople and this increases retention.

Overview of differences

	Transactional	Consultative
Type of sale	Standard/commodity	Strategic, often transformational
Current status	Less common because of e-commerce and procurement sophistication	More common because of increasing complexity of businesses and globalisation
Salesperson	Telesales Web Order takers, sometimes face to face	Face to face Subject matter expert Problem solver
Sales cycle	Can be quick	Likely to take quite some time (often several meetings)
Knowledge	Customer probably knows what they want	Customer open to education, probably does not know solution or even that there is a problem
Focus	Features and benefits	Matching needs with bespoke solutions
Sale	Small and numerous	Large and few
Price	Critical and central to buying decision	Collaborative and based around trading concessions
Prospecting	Critical and short-term	Important and slow-burn
Procurement department	Sometimes involved	Often involved
Relationship with buyer	Often short-term and transactional in nature	Likely to be long-term and collaborative

Communicating with prospects and customers

In Chapter 11 of this book we talked about the importance of building connection and establishing credibility with your prospects. Often, this is still built through face to face communication. However, the reality of the new sales environment in which so many of us now operate is that we have to communicate **remotely**. This will include telephone contact and email and, more recently, video conferencing and virtual meetings. A lot of salespeople involved in consultative selling may have already used tools such as Skype to communicate with prospects and clients and may have either hosted or attended a 'virtual' seminar. So:

- What do we need to remember with regard to body language when we communicate remotely?
- What are some of the characteristics of remote selling and how do we need to think differently in order to sell and maintain existing relationships?

Used correctly, tools such as email and video conferencing can be highly effective. They make it easier to connect with prospects and customers wherever they are, and they can reduce the costs of travel and time, enabling us to be more efficient. But we must pay attention to some basic 'rules' if these tools are to add value and be effective rather than leaving prospects and customers with a less than positive view of us. As with telephone and face to face meetings, we need to be proactive in how we use them to make the best use of the opportunities they present.

Before we look more closely at communicating remotely, it is worth remembering the league table of effective communication:

1 Face to face

There is still nothing better than real (non-virtual) face to face meetings to maximise the opportunity to build rapport and demonstrate credibility. Let's focus on body language. Body language conveys a lot of the meaning in communications and meetings and is the most important factor in creating a chemistry with the other person. We all make meaning out of first impressions.

Within a few seconds, snap decisions are made as to whether we are liked, trusted or credible. People are more likely to believe what they see than what they hear, which is why we must pay attention to body language. The overwhelming majority of the meaning that is taken from an interaction is derived from our body language and the non-verbal aspects of what we are saying. Your impact is judged on how you look, how you sound, and least of all on *what* you are saying. Remember, it works both ways so you need to be aware of:

people are more likely to believe what they see than what they hear

- Your own body language – the messages you are giving out.
- The body language of others – so that you can react appropriately.

There are two essential things to look out for when reading body language, either in yourself or in other people.

- Comfort or discomfort?
- Open or closed body language?

James Borg, in his book *Body Language: How to Know What's Really Being Said*, says that paying attention to these issues throughout your interaction will make you highly attuned to the important messages you are both transmitting and receiving when you are involved in any aspect of selling. You need to ask, what is being displayed?:

Pay keen attention to the following:

- 'Closed' body language is a cluster of gestures, movements and postures that bring the body in on itself. For example, poor eye contact, crossing arms or legs repeatedly, or running your hands through your hair. If there is a 'cluster' then others will instinctively feel repelled.

- If a person is comfortable they exhibit 'open' body language, which is welcoming, relaxed and attentive. If somebody is positive and open, their hands are usually in view, possibly with palms open, their legs and posture are free and easy and eye contact is good.

So, ask yourself a few questions. What signals am I sending out? How might they be interpreted by the other person? Are they what I intended? Am I showing signs of discomfort, boredom, fear, nervousness or hostility? The first step is to recognise negative body language that delivers the wrong message – then you can consciously change it for more positive signals. Chapter 11 covers this in more detail.

> *'The average person looks without seeing, listens without hearing, touches without feeling, moves without physical awareness and talks without thinking.'* – Leonardo da Vinci, Italian artist and polymath

2 Video conferencing

While still providing a visual element, video conferencing is unlikely to be as effective as a face to face meeting. If you follow the tips opposite you can maximise its effectiveness and avoid some of the common pitfalls.

3 Telephone

If you cannot have a face to face meeting or video conference then a telephone call can also be really effective. Without the visual element you lose an important aspect of conveying meaning in your communication, so you need to pay attention to your words and voice tone to ensure you get the right message across.

4 Email

With email you, literally, just have the words – so use them wisely. I don't know of many great relationships that have been built by email, so use the other communication channels wherever possible.

Communicating remotely

Let's look at video conferencing and email communication in more detail and give you some top tips.

Video conferencing

Video conferencing is becoming an increasingly popular way of communicating in the sales process. As the market becomes more global it is often easier, faster and less expensive to use this technology than arrange a more 'traditional' meeting.

While you retain a visual element to the communication there are some important distinctions that you need to take account of to make the most of the new approach. This approach often does not convey non-verbal communication as well as a real face to face meeting would. So, whether you use Skype or an alternative conferencing package, the following 10 top tips should prove useful:

1 **What should I wear?** Dress as if you were holding the meeting in the prospect's office. If that means you would have worn a suit, then wear a suit for the video conference. If you are at home, resist the urge to 'half dress' by wearing a dress shirt but shorts under the desk – it would be embarrassing if the camera fell over or you needed to get up to fetch something that you needed! Also, light, solid-coloured clothing often looks best on video. Greys and blues often work well because they bring out healthy skin tones and avoid distraction. It helps to avoid colours that match your

skin or hair tones too closely as these may tend to wash out your natural colouration. Bright reds, greens or oranges and tops with close stripes are also best avoided as they sometimes come across as either harsh or distracting on video.

2. **Check your technology**. Part of the success of holding an online meeting or video conference in sales depends on taking the time to check your technology works *before* the meeting takes place. There is nothing more frustrating to a prospect than having to wait while you sort out your technical issues.
3. **Have a clear agenda**. As with a face to face meeting, it is important to respect people's time. You should prepare an agenda, circulate it in advance and ensure that all participants are aware of the timings and objectives of the meeting.
4. **Have clear ground rules**. Video conferencing is still new to many. Be clear on what your expectations are in the meeting and how you will handle things such as questions. Be mindful that there is sometimes a delay in the sound and/or video, so it is not as easy for it to re-create the natural flow of conversation that takes place in a conventional face to face meeting.
5. **Look into the camera**. Sometimes the camera is situated above (or below) the screen where you are viewing the other person in the video conference. If you are looking at them on the screen then they are seeing your eyes looking down rather than at them and this does not contribute to building a sense of real connection between you. Focus on trying to get eye contact.
6. **Consider the background**. Think about what the other person or people will see. Is it just you? Your desk? People walking behind you? The background can serve to distract people if too much is going on. Also, if they can see your desk, ensure it is tidy!

7. **Be aware of noise**. Sound quality is even more important than video quality. It's surprising just how much noise we 'tune out' of our daily environment. It may not distract us, but a noisy fan, a computer 'pinging' with a new email or outside sounds through an open window can be very distracting to the other people in the conference. Do what you need to eliminate these distractions.
8. **Stay focused on the meeting**. It is easy to get distracted in video conferences and other forms of online meeting, so avoid this and keep focused on the meeting itself. Do not attempt to multi-task! This extends to ensuring you are not disturbed during the meeting by your mobile, people coming into your office or anything else.
9. **Think about your communication**. Even on a video conference a lot of non-verbal communication is lost. Your communication needs to be clear. Showing empathy, acknowledging feelings, clarifying and summarising are all very important techniques in video conferencing. They ensure you do what you can to develop rapport, minimise the chance of misunderstanding and demonstrate your active listening.
10. **Follow up**. Make sure you follow up immediately after a video conference with an email. Be clear on what actions were agreed and who had what responsibilities.

Email communication

Even though email has been a fixture of our business world now for many years, we see it either overused or used ineffectively. It seems to have developed from a really useful means of offline clarification and confirmation of details into something that is, at worst, irritating, frustrating and ineffective. Our speed of response has encouraged others to think of us as being 'immediately available', and most of us have had the experience of receiving an email into our inbox only to be followed two minutes later by a phone call from the sender asking if we had received their email as we had not yet responded! If it is that important – *pick up the phone* and don't use email!

OK, rant over. Here are six top tips for the effective use of email:

1. **Have a purpose**. Know why you are sending the mail – and let the recipient know the reason too.
2. **Choose who to include in the address and cc lines**. Resist the urge to send the mail to too many people. I had a colleague who once told us all that if he was not the only name in the addressee line he would ignore the mail because he figured the other person or people in the addressee line would handle it. If his name was in the cc line he would also ignore it because he figured we were sending it for our benefit (to protect ourselves) rather than for his benefit.
3. **Think of the recipient**. What is their style of communication? Try and match this with the style of your mail as it will help build a little more rapport than simply sending a 'stream of consciousness' message. For example, do they like the big picture or more detail?
4. **Finish with a strong call to action**. Be clear and succinct – what do you want the recipient to do as a result of the mail?
5. **Set email expectations**. Help people understand your approach to email. How often do you check mails, how quickly do you look to respond to emails and what should people do if they need a faster response? I have a friend who simply does not respond to email – it certainly encourages me to call him instead and we often get a lot more done as a result.
6. **Do not make it your 'standard' way of communicating**. Email is no substitute for picking up the telephone.

Effective selling includes making the best use of your time. Tools such as video conferencing and email are all part of your toolbox. If used appropriately they can be a significant help. Used without sufficient thought, however, they can trip you up and reduce the quality of the relationship between your prospects and yourself.

brilliant recap

In this chapter we have identified:

- There are essentially two models of selling.
- Transactional selling is often used when there is a 'standard' product or service to sell.
- Consultative selling is focused on developing long-term relationships and is often used for selling bespoke solutions.
- There is no substitute for face to face meetings but, when these are not practical, other technologies can be useful – as long as you observe some basic 'rules' that are often overlooked.
- The overwhelming majority of the meaning that is taken from an interaction is derived from our body language and the non-verbal aspects of our communication. Pay attention to your own body language and that of others. Remember, it's not what you think that matters ... it's what you communicate.

We can't sell in isolation – we need a potential buyer! But what are the needs of the modern buyer and what do they think of us? That's where we are headed next ...

CHAPTER 16

The modern buyer

In order to understand how people responsible for corporate buying decisions feel about their interactions with salespeople, DDI (the selection and development specialists, **www.ddiworld.com**) conducted a major global study of corporate buyers. Survey respondents included 2,705 corporate buyers and those involved with the buying process across six countries (Australia, Canada, France, Germany, the UK and USA) and representatives of a wide range of industries, job levels and age groups.

DDI specifically wanted to know how these people view their buyer–seller relationships and asked buyers a series of questions that included:

- What qualities do they value in a salesperson?
- Have their expectations of salespeople changed?
- What value do salespeople provide to buying organisations?

> *'He who buys need have 100 eyes, but one's enough for him that sells the stuff.'* – Benjamin Franklin, US statesman

---

brilliant exercise

Take a moment to think of at least one of your current buyers.

1. Write down what you think they want out of the relationship between them and you and the business you represent.
2. Write down what you imagine they think of you.

Maybe you have written a glowing self-reference; and maybe that is fair. The stark reality is that what buyers really think about salespeople does not make particularly comfortable reading, according to this study.

many buyers have a poor perception of salespeople

The research suggested that many buyers have a poor perception of salespeople. Here are some of the comments from buyers about salespeople captured by the researchers:

- 'Unwilling to listen.'
- 'Won't take no for an answer.'
- 'Lacking knowledge about their products.'
- 'More interested in commission than what I need.'
- 'Doesn't understand my circumstances.'

Hardly a ringing endorsement!

The move away from transactional selling means that salespeople should be adding more value throughout the whole sales process. However, when buyers were asked to describe their perceptions of the sales process, the most common description, across all countries, was that the sales process is 'a necessary evil'. Only 6 per cent rated the sales profession 'excellent'. Buyers in the UK provided the lowest ratings, with 53 per cent rating sales 'Poor' or 'Fair'. However, overall, 54 per cent of buyers said 'Yes' to this question – would you consider your sales contacts to be business partners? So, over half are now getting more value from the relationship, although there were regional differences. In the UK, for instance, only 42 per cent answered 'Yes'.

only 6 per cent rated the sales profession 'excellent'

There is a positive intent articulated by buyers. For example, more than 90 per cent of customers would like their salesperson to be more of a resource to them. More worryingly perhaps is that over two-thirds of buyers believe salespeople's expertise is getting worse.

The key finding that stood out was this:

- 61 per cent of buyers said sales representatives were transaction-orientated only and did not understand customer needs.

While many organisations, sales managers and salespeople understand the necessity to reach beyond the transaction model, many buyers feel differently. The report highlights the growing gap between what buyers want from salespeople and what they are routinely given in terms of service and expertise.

So let us start looking at ways in which salespeople, across all market sectors and across the globe, can really make a difference. There *are* salespeople out there adding value, offering great service, aligning what they offer with their customers' requirements and making great money! Our survey of 300 salespeople (**www.brilliant-selling.com**) suggests that these people are open to change, flexible and thoroughly professional. They adapt their approach and meet the evolving needs of the people who make the decisions.

What buyers want

So what are the expectations of the **buyer**? What questions do they have as they decide which partners to choose? These are 20 key questions that are on buyers' minds:

What are you offering

1. What is your product/service?
2. How does your product/service fit with my business and my current business outcomes?

3. How will your product/service help me now and in the future?
4. How can you guarantee the quality of your product or service?

Legitimacy of your business

5. What sort of reputation does your company have?
6. What experience does your company have in my market?
7. What would others in my business think of your product/service?

Competition

8. Why should I buy from you and not someone else?

Price versus value

9. Why should I pay your price?
10. Can I make sufficient margin by buying your product/service?

Timing

11. Do I really need to buy this now?
12. Can I wait to buy your product?
13. What would be the implications if I did wait to buy?

You

14. What relevant experience do you have in my market/business?
15. What do first impressions tell me about you, your product/service and your company?
16. What would others in my organisation think of you?
17. Am I likely to trust you?

18 How will you help me achieve my own personal goals?

19 Do I like you?

20 Can I see you as a potential business partner in the future?

What buyers fear

Just as salespeople are paid on results, so, increasingly, are buyers. They have real fears that we need to identify and meet. These will include:

- The fear of paying too much.
- The fear of change.
- The fear of being left behind.
- The fear of loss.
- The fear of not knowing enough about what they are buying.
- The fear of not hitting their procurement targets.

What can you offer?

Our job as a salesperson is to answer the buyers' questions and address their fears. And so the ultimate question for any buyer is: 'Why should I buy from you?'.

> there is plenty of competition out there

There is plenty of competition out there and if we are not able to answer this basic question with a degree of lucidity, we will struggle. People buy results, so what result can you offer?

Most buyers, and this goes for consumers as well as professionals, will go through this kind of decision-making process before they buy anything:

- I'm OK: I have what I need.
- I am dissatisfied in some way – what I have is no longer OK.

- I decide to do something.
- I do some research – what are the options?
- I have some concerns – are these resolvable?
- I buy.
- I convince myself it was the right thing to do.

It's worth remembering this process as you go through the stages of a sale with a buyer. So let us focus on a practical application for you:

brilliant exercise

Take one of your key clients or prospects and put yourself in the buyer's shoes.

1. Go through the list of 20 questions above and decide which of these are likely to be on your buyers' minds.
2. What other questions might they have about your particular product/service?
3. As a buyer, attempt to answer the questions.
4. What fears do they have?
5. Finally – take your time to decide what actions you can take so that you build more trust and either sell for the first time or win more business.

There is a fair amount of consistency across regions as to what buyers are looking for from their salespeople. Of course, they want respect, a sensible level of support and advice when it is appropriate. The table below outlines the nine key qualities that buyers are seeking from a sales partner, identified by DDI, and shows the most important.

What are the top three qualities you value the most in a salesperson?

	Global	Australia	Canada	France	Germany	UK	USA
Product or service advice	67%	70%	64%	72%	76%	58%	59%
Market knowledge	44%	42%	44%	36%	58%	41%	41%
Trust	43%	47%	57%	40%	15%	49%	51%
Pricing/price negotiation	41%	47%	44%	35%	29%	49%	45%
Relationship building	31%	34%	34%	24%	30%	33%	32%
Delivery expediting	30%	23%	22%	40%	47%	26%	24%
Customer & supplier interface	24%	21%	22%	20%	36%	24%	23%
Business advice	8%	5%	6%	15%	7%	6%	7%
ROI analysis	4%	1%	2%	13%	1%	1%	4%

Take a careful look at the above table. Now, all salespeople are taught that people will only buy if there is a match between what someone is selling and what another wants or needs. So the above table is one of the most important parts of *Brilliant Selling*. This table represents what your buyers want.

brilliant exercise

Take some time over the following exercise – commit yourself to researching and getting clear about where your strengths and possible weaknesses are.

Your job here is to complete the grid so that you have a good sense of where you are now in your own development. If you are a sales manager, get your sales team to complete the task.

1. For a complete picture, first of all do your own self-analysis.
2. Next ask your sales manager to complete the grid.
3. Finally, find at least one trusted customer and ask them to complete the grid.

Score between 0 and 5 (0 = I never deliver, 1 = very occasionally deliver, 2 = quite often deliver, 3= often deliver, 4= deliver well, 5 = deliver excellently).

	YOUR SCORE	SALES MANAGER	TRUSTED CLIENT
Product or service advice			
Market knowledge			
Trust			
Pricing/price negotiation			
Relationship building			
Delivery expediting			
Customer and supplier interface			
Business advice			
ROI analysis			

- What do you notice?
- Where are the similarities? These will probably be your core strengths.
- In what areas are your lower average scores? These are likely to be your weaknesses.
- Finally, ask yourself this: What can I do in the next three months that is not reliant on any external factors but my own effort, which will improve my weak areas? Then commit yourself to taking action right now.

brilliant recap

We have covered quite a lot of ground here and so by now you should have a much greater sense of the identity of the modern buyer and what they want. What buyers want to see in salespeople can perhaps best be summed up by one DDI respondent in France who said: 'Truth, sincerity, knowledge of product and understanding of my needs as a client'. Is this what you (and your team) deliver regularly right now?

Key elements uncovered in this chapter include:

- Research suggests that many buyers have a low opinion of salespeople.
- Only 6 per cent rated the sales profession 'excellent'.
- Buyers want answers about your offering, the legitimacy of your business, how you stack up against the competition, your price vs. the value you offer, when to buy and you as an individual. Their key question is: why should I buy from you?'
- The four qualities buyers most look for from salespeople are product advice, market knowledge, trust and a good price.

So now we know what buyers think of us as salespeople and what they want, how do we influence them to buy from us? We need to become really good at prospecting.

Prospecting with purpose

In some organisations a salesperson is not expected to do any prospecting at all – this is all done via the marketing or telesales departments. In most businesses, and certainly if you run your own business, prospecting is critical. And yet it is amazing how salespeople find excuses not to prospect. The root of this failure to focus on prospecting consistently could be:

it is amazing how salespeople find excuses not to prospect

- Fear of rejection.
- Poor time management.
- Dislike of the process.
- Not confident about what to do and what to say.

Maybe you have another favourite?

> '*Where oil is first found is in the minds of men.*' – Wallace Pratt, US pioneer petroleum geologist

The act of connecting with your prospects can be done in a number of ways. Prospecting is not just about cold calling and cold calling may or may not be part of the way you prospect. Some sales commentators have suggested that cold calling is dead, but we are aware of a number of companies who are continuing to invest in their cold-calling strategies.

So let us accept prospecting can be tough, uncomfortable and sometimes disheartening. This chapter gives you some key guidelines within which to work. These ideas are taken from modelling people who are successful at this element of the sales process – known in sales circles, somewhat archaically, as 'the hunters'.

brilliant definition

In the broad sense, **prospecting** refers to exploration – you could be prospecting for valuable minerals and ores, such as gold, silver, or oil. In sales, prospecting is the search for potential customers.

brilliant exercise

When you think of sales prospecting, what pops up in your mind?

What stops us focusing more time on prospecting, and performing the task well?

Research suggests that there are two key things that will determine how successful you are at prospecting: attitude and action.

You need to develop a healthy and positive attitude to prospecting and you need to take positive action to support it. The truth of the matter is that if we do not prospect, we do not win new accounts and our sales can stagnate or fall sharply, because there is one certainty in sales – however good we are, we *will* lose customers. It is just in the nature of business – companies fail, they merge or are acquired, or your contact is replaced. Change happens. Equally, anyone in sales can fall into the trap of complacency when their sales are good. You may have heard the expression 'feast or famine'. To avoid this cycle you must continue to prospect, even when sales are good.

Myths of sales prospecting

There are many myths around sales prospecting, so let us dispel some of these and then look at how to prospect with purpose.

Myth 1: Prospecting is the same thing as sales

It's not about selling at this stage – it is about discarding people and organisations who do not fit your criteria for doing business. You are looking for the 'gold', for organisations that qualify to get to the next stage. In most sales scenarios the key qualification questions are:

- Will my product or service solve a problem for them?
- Can they afford it?
- Are they willing to spend?

The job of prospecting is to find qualified leads – people who are able to buy your product/service. Only after this process is complete should the selling begin.

Myth 2: Prospecting is a numbers game

Old-school thinking suggests you need to contact hundreds of people. Not necessarily! We do a lot of work with law firms and there are thousands of law firms in the UK. Our best prospecting campaign (including advertising and email) was to only 60 firms and we got 14 strong leads. So, it is about quality, not quantity.

Myth 3: Prospecting is time-intensive

Done well, prospecting can take just a few minutes. Do not waste time on people unmotivated or unable to buy. You may decide to contact them again at a later stage, but avoid pressing for more contact or interest if there is none! Remember to focus on the 'gold'.

remember to focus on the 'gold'

If you prospected competently for two hours per week you would start seeing great results within a month.

Myth 4: Scripts simply do not work

Many salespeople prospect on the telephone or face to face without any script or basic framework, but scripting is essential for a successful prospecting campaign. It allows you to test which key benefits and qualifying questions work. Of course, you need to personalise the script and make sure it sounds natural, but create one script initially and change it as required, depending on what is working.

Myth 5: You need to 'close' them on the appointment

Many sales representatives focus too much time on getting the appointment and later wonder why so many prospects then cancel. People do not like to say no, so they say yes and then cancel later by email, or just exit stage left at the agreed time of the appointment.

An alternative is to send prospects some information first and follow up later, or tell them something new or of value on the first call. Either of these tactics adds an extra stage, but is more likely to produce better-qualified initial appointments.

The prospecting process

So now we are done with the myths, how do we prospect successfully? Here is a process that works.

1 Identify prospects

Your prospects may be blindingly obvious – if you are selling gym equipment it may well be worth contacting local sports centres. If you sell wine, off-licences may be a good bet. However, with many products and services the potential end user is not always crystal clear. So you may have to start by identifying your prospecting criteria. With whom do you want to do business? You will either be identifying a business or an individual. This table will help you build a profile of your intended prospect.

Business	Individual
What market?	What demographic?
What turnover?	What income?
What geographical area?	What geographical area?
What role in business?	What job roles?
What specific business?	What pastimes?
Existing or new users?	What family?

Then go out there and find these businesses or individuals; you may well also be employing marketing tools to help you in this journey.

2 Plan and research your prospects

Once you have identified a prospect, it is critical to do some research before first contact.

Let us assume you are working in business-to-business sales. In order to make a favourable first impression, you need to identify some of the following about any prospect:

- Culture.
- Obvious problems or challenges.
- Principal areas of business that would benefit from your product/service.
- Is the business growing, stagnating?
- Merging or restructuring?

- Cutting costs, laying off staff?
- What are the market trends?
- What factors will make your product/service a 'must have' rather than a 'nice to have'?

Distil your research into what you want to say when you speak on the telephone – focus on these questions to yourself:

- Can you help?
- How?
- Have you done this before?
- What value did you bring?
- Do you have a case study or testimonial to support this?
- What is their likely spend with you?
- Who is the right person to contact?

Identify a number of **valid business reasons** for a call – these could include a restructuring initiative, a new purchase, redundancies, or a new opening.

brilliant exercise

What valid business reasons (VBRs) can you think of for a prospect wanting to talk to you?

Think about whether you really want the prospects as customers:

- Does their profile match your ideal profile of a customer?
- What is their likely ability to meet your target price points?
- Will they have the ability to buy your minimum quantities?
- Who is the competition? What does this tell us?

You will then be in a position to contact them. Options that were identified by over 300 successful salespeople in our Brilliant Selling survey (**www.brilliant-selling.com**) included:

- pitching up at a customer's premises
- sending samples
- an introductory email
- direct mail
- simply making a telephone call
- getting a referral from a customer or supplier
- using a telesales expert
- specific targeted campaigns
- hosting a seminar
- speaking at a conference
- PR
- trade shows
- networking events.

3 Plan the initial telephone call

In many business scenarios your first contact with a prospect will be on the telephone. When you call a company you should talk about them and their business, not you and your company.

What are you going to say? Identify the structure and content for your call and ideally find time to rehearse what you are going to say.

Create a basic script. This will help you measure your success and, paradoxically, will free you up to focus on any response, because you already know what you are going to say.

Think about any objections you might meet – what are they likely to be and how would you handle them?

Possible objection	Ways of meeting objection

4 Get into a resourceful state

Ensure you are in a resourceful state to make the initial telephone call. This is key. (There is more information on this in Part 3 – Your power to influence.)

For the purposes of this call, try some of these ideas:

- Say positive things to yourself – the prospect will like me/the company will benefit from my services/I want to find out more about them/the PA is a gate-opener not a gatekeeper.
- Stretch and feel physically relaxed.
- Stand up – you will feel better and more in control.
- Smile – it relaxes you and your voice.
- Use music – play a favourite energising tune.
- Take a stroll.
- Speak to someone you like.

5 Make the initial call to the organisation

Your first call to a prospect could well be with a PA, or you might get lucky and make it direct to the prospect.

Your initial call structure with a PA or gatekeeper might look like this:

- Greet – your name, position and company.
- State your valid business reason(s) for the call.
- Check he/she is the right person.
- Request a brief telephone call when it is convenient, and book.
- Thank them.

Treat gatekeepers and PAs with immense respect. Explain to them the proposition as though they are the decision maker. It is surprising how many bosses trust the opinions of their PA. Treat them as a potential ally and not an obstacle. Treating them as an obstacle is a self-fulfilling prophecy.

Build rapport with whomever you speak. You can do this easily by remembering that it is not what you say but how you say it that will have the most impact. So, focus on how the person you are influencing speaks: the speed, volume and tone of the voice as well as how they breathe. Also, listen for what they say – and match their language. Remember that on the telephone we only have the voice and the words on which to focus.

listen for what they say – and match language

6 Make the initial call to the prospective buyer

All of the above is also relevant when you make the initial call to the prospect. Remember that here your key objective is to get an appointment with the prospect. Ideally call in the morning, and not on a Monday or Friday.

Your call structure might look like this:

- Greet – your name, position and company.
- State your valid business reason(s) for the call – reiterate what worked with the initial call.
- Draw a link with the PA or other person in their business.
- Identify what some of the key challenges are for the prospect.
- Use qualification questions to test their level of interest.
- Define one key benefit for meeting with you, from the perspective of the prospect – use their language and include benefit statements so you make it compelling!
- Give one case study or testimonial to support the above, if required.
- Request a meeting – give a couple of alternatives and confirm the time and date.
- Thank them.

7 Follow up all calls

Always follow up telephone conversations with emails confirming what was said and agreed. This will improve your credibility and will be good for people who like to reflect on conversations.

If the prospect has agreed to meet you, then you have momentum and can focus on the first face to face meeting.

brilliant recap

Certainly, prospecting can be tough at times, and yet there is the prospect of mining some real gold. If you have to prospect as part of your sales role you need to:

- Forget the myths of prospecting – they are just excuses for not taking action.
- Adopt a great attitude.
- Focus on the activity on a regular basis.
- Create and follow a tried and tested process, which will ensure prospects become buyers as quickly as possible. It is likely to include these steps: identify your prospects, research them, plan your initial call, get into a resourceful state, make the calls and follow up.

Adopt these four principles and you will get yourself some face to face meetings fairly rapidly!

Initial meeting(s) with the prospect

You have made the calls and got the appointment – now is your chance to find out what your prospect wants and to start selling yourself as a problem solver and credible business partner.

Depending on your market and your approach (transactional or consultative), there could be just the one meeting or several meetings before any decision is made about a purchase. It is possible your first meeting may even end up with an order. This is often the case with the FMCG (fast-moving consumer goods) market.

If it is possible, include one other person (connected to the sale in some way) in this first (and, ideally, subsequent) meeting; '2-up' selling has some real benefits – it means it can be more interesting for the buyer, it relieves pressure and it can be a more creative meeting. It follows the old adage that two heads are better than one!

In this first meeting make sure you add some value in some way. Come armed with new information on the prospect's business or the market. In our Brilliant Selling survey (**www.brilliant-selling.com**) 92 per cent of successful salespeople who responded confirmed that they attempt to educate the customer on a regular basis.

> *You don't get paid for the hour. You get paid for the* ***value*** *you bring to the hour.'* – Jim Rohn, US entrepreneur, author and motivational speaker

Think carefully about these specific points before your next meeting with a prospective buyer:

Do more research

Buyers get bored with boring questions. They will either inwardly groan or outwardly yawn if you come up with questions such as:

- So – how's business?
- Can you tell me about how you are organised?
- What's happening in the market?

You should know the answers to these situational questions! You can only know this if you do the research – use the internet, read the market journals, speak to people in your organisation and come armed with facts. Buyers get turned off if they are asked questions that do not add value to their thinking.

Be prepared for all meetings and do some digging to find out what is happening in a business.

In a first meeting with a new prospect, these are the minimum things you may need to know:

- Facts and figures on turnover, margins and profitability.
- Organisational structure.
- History of the business.
- Recent important internal news – acquisitions, etc.
- Basic job overview of the buyer.

Be patient

One key issue we have seen with many of the sales forces with whom we have worked is that often salespeople give up too quickly. Would you buy first time from someone you had not met before? It once took me 12 months to convert an FMCG account, but their first order was my biggest of the quarter! We recently won some business from a top-15 accountancy firm after 18 months and five meetings. The first order was for well over £17,000.

In case you have not been convinced yourself of this fact yet, allow us to share with you some statistics that should scare the living daylights out of salespeople:

- 48 per cent of salespeople never follow up with a prospect
- 25 per cent of salespeople make a second contact and stop
- 12 per cent of salespeople only make three contacts and stop.

So – only 15 per cent of salespeople make more than three contacts. What does this mean, then? Well, it means 85 per cent of salespeople consistently waste golden opportunities to sell!

only 15 per cent of salespeople make more than three contacts

Because ...

- 2 per cent of sales are made on the first contact
- 3 per cent of sales are made on the second contact
- 5 per cent of sales are made on the third contact
- 10 per cent of sales are made on the fourth contact
- 80 per cent of sales are made on the fifth to twelfth contact.

So, if you are like almost half of all salespeople and make no more than one follow-up to your prospects, you are leaving 98 per cent of your income on the table for someone else to come along and pick up.

80 per cent of sales are made on the fifth to twelfth contact

Offer insight

We have mentioned a number of times in this book the importance of increasing your personal brand value and becoming a Key Person of Influence (KPI). A great opportunity to be seen immediately as a KPI is to offer or create insight as early as possible to a new prospect. You can create insight by asking questions that raise awareness. What we mean by offering 'insight' is providing information to the prospect (or client, because offering insights can be used at all stages of the sales process) that they may find of value. This might include:

- Information on market trends.
- Regional variations that have an impact on their business.
- New or relevant legislation.
- Feedback from an external source about their product or service.
- Examples of what has worked well for other clients.

brilliant recap

Here is a summary of what really matters in a first meeting:

- Always add value – in every meeting!
- If possible bring someone else to your first meeting(s).
- Do the research – buyers are easily bored and often underwhelmed by salespeople.
- Be patient – it is not always possible to strike gold first time!
- Consciously seek to offer or create insight for the prospect.

If you do a great job in the initial meeting with the prospect you will earn the right to find out how you can help them – to find out their wants and needs.

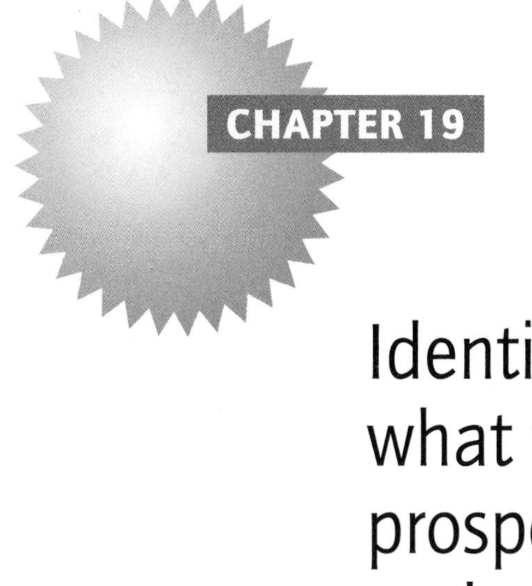

Identifying what the prospect wants and needs

Whether you are involved in transactional or consultative selling, it is imperative that you spend time identifying and agreeing what it is that your prospect and their organisation wants and needs. Avoid selling too quickly. People do not like being sold to. Do you? Usually we become defensive if we know someone is attempting to sell something. So – stop it! Build the relationship, develop trust, listen carefully and keep your overt selling to yourself!

> *'You will get all you want in life if you help enough other people get what they want.'* – Zig Ziglar, author, salesperson and motivational speaker

At this stage you are looking to identify what the buyer needs and wants. What are the distinctions?

brilliant definitions

A **need** is something you have to have, something you cannot do without to survive.

A **want** is something you would like to have. It has emotional pull. And we cannot emphasise enough – a want pulls the emotional strings of desire.

Wants relate to emotions, whereas **needs** relate to something definitive within the specific business.

Generally, people buy what they want. They often don't buy what they need. It may be that what they want is what they think they need, but they could be very wrong about what they need. Beware! Prospects often do not know what they want. This may be because they do not know what is available. As Henry Ford suggested, 'If I had asked my customers what they wanted they'd have said a faster horse!'. Buyers sometimes need educating in order that they want the right thing (which, hopefully, is your product/service).

Do you use a fabric conditioner in your house? Very few people were crying out for this product before it was launched by Unilever in the UK in 1969. Now, most modern washing machines have a dispenser that can add liquid fabric softener to the load of laundry automatically, and the market is worth £1 billion per year.

Do you remember when an Iraqi journalist (Muntazar al-Zaidi) threw a shoe at George W. Bush in December 2008? He was subsequently imprisoned. Ramazan Baydan, the owner of an Istanbul shoe company, was inundated with orders and had to recruit another 100 staff to cope with the demand. Many people buying probably did not need a new pair of shoes, but they certainly wanted one!

SPIN® selling

We can identify the needs and wants of prospects by asking questions and listening actively (for more on this see Part 3 – Your power to influence). Specifically, when you are in the needs identification stage it is sensible to remember the SPIN® model. British research psychologist Neil Rackham developed the SPIN selling system, and his company, Huthwaite Inc., has taught the system to hundreds of corporations worldwide. Developing the system involved 12 years of research and analysis of 35,000 sales situations.

At the heart of the system, explained in Rackham's book *SPIN Selling*, is a precisely defined sequence of four question types that enables the salesperson to move the conversation logically from exploring the customer's needs to designing solutions, or, in Rackham's terms, to uncover implied needs and develop them into explicit needs that you, the salesperson, can resolve. SPIN is the best-researched sales methodology around and is modelled on what Brilliant Salespeople do on a regular basis to identify what the prospect wants and needs. It is especially useful in complex or big-ticket sales, or if you use a consultative approach to selling.

The template can be used with both prospects and existing customers.

Here are the four types of questions identified by Rackham:

1 Situation questions

Every good seller begins the sales call by assessing the business terrain, by asking questions to clarify the customer's current situation. So situation questions are essential to gather information, but here is the surprise. Huthwaite's research found that, as valuable as they are, situation questions can be overused by inexperienced salespeople.

In big sales, minimise the small talk and focus on finding background detail that can be used to make sense of the buyer's business situation. This is about understanding the wider context of the prospect's business, before you zoom into the details.

Do not ask a question to elicit information that you could easily have obtained before beginning the call, during the research phase. And remember, when overused these questions *bore* the customer.

Examples of situation questions:

- 'What's your position?'
- 'Who are your current suppliers?'
- 'Other than yourself, who are the key decision makers?'
- 'What is your vision for your business?'

brilliant exercise

What sort of situation questions do you or could you ask?

2 Problem questions

Questions that are designed to identify a customer's problem are more often asked by experienced salespeople. The more experienced you become, the more you *want* to uncover difficulties. You start to understand that customer difficulties present you with an opportunity to be of service. One caveat, though: Huthwaite's research suggests that the effectiveness of these questions is inversely proportional to the size of the sale under consideration. They are most effective in smaller-ticket transactions.

> the more experienced you become, the more you *want* to uncover difficulties

A trap here is to dive straight into presenting the benefits of what you are selling. Going straight to the sales pitch will simply raise objections.

Examples of problem questions:

- 'What are the key challenges facing you in your business right now?'
- 'How satisfied are you with your current suppliers?'
- 'What kind of obstacles are you facing in this area?'
- 'How do these challenges manifest themselves?'

brilliant exercise

What sort of problem questions do you or could you ask?

3 Implication questions

These are questions about the 'effects, consequences or implications of the customer's problems'. They are strongly linked to success in larger-ticket sales and yet they are more difficult to phrase than either situation questions or problem questions. But they are essential to moving larger sales forward.

Instead of telling customers the problem they have (which is also likely to raise objections), the goal is now to get them to see (and feel!) the problem. By being asked questions that draw out the implications of the problem, the buyer gets to feel the pain that will drive them towards your product/service.

People are motivated by moving away from pain or towards pleasure (for more on this go to Part 1 – You). These questions are intended to make the problem more acute for the buyer.

Examples of implication questions:

- 'What effect does this (problem) have?'
- 'What sort of risk would this constitute if nothing was done about it?'
- 'What does this reduction in income mean for growth?'
- 'What would happen if you did nothing?'

brilliant exercise

What sort of implication questions do you or could you ask?

4 Need-payoff questions

Need-payoff questions are linked to success in more complex sales. They can be especially useful when you are talking to top decision makers (or those who will influence them). These questions focus the customer's attention on the solution rather than the problem, and they encourage them (with your assistance) to outline the benefits that your solution will provide their company. The focus is on the 'pleasure' of solving the problem. A good need-payoff question both pre-empts objections and enlists customer buy-in.

Examples of need-payoff questions:

- 'Is it important for you to solve the problem?'
- 'How do you think a faster supply chain solution would help you?'
- 'What kind of solution would best fit your current needs?'
- 'What sort of benefits would you see if something was done about this?'

---

brilliant exercise

What sort of need-payoff questions do you or could you ask?

How successful people sell

> The logic of the SPIN process is common sense

The logic of the SPIN process is common sense. The problem with common sense is that it is often not that common!

As Rackham acknowledges, the SPIN model is not a revolutionary discovery. Putting these four questions together in an orderly sequence, Rackham gives the following thumbnail definition of the SPIN selling model. It is simply 'the way most successful people sell on a good day when the call is going well'.

Make your prospect feel that you care. Make it easy for the customer to order. Do not focus on selling, but identify the challenges and issues in the business and ask questions that turn up the heat and give the buyer an opportunity to see there would be benefits to addressing the problem.

> do not focus on selling but identify the challenges and issues in the business

brilliant recap

This final chapter in the section on buyers and prospects is pivotal. If you are unable to identify and agree what a buyer wants, you are in danger of becoming a desperate salesperson who tries to position your product/service as a solution to all known problems. Here is a summary of what is covered in this chapter:

- There is a difference between wants and needs. Buyers buy what they want.
- You can uncover what a buyer wants and needs through carefully structured questioning and active listening.
- The sequence for asking these questions is SPIN (situation, problem, implication, need-payoff), which models the questions that successful salespeople ask.

Identifying the wants and needs of the prospect is critical, but to secure the sale you will need to present your proposal or product/service effectively. There are a number of aspects of this important element of the sales process that you must pay attention to. We focus on these in the next part of this book.

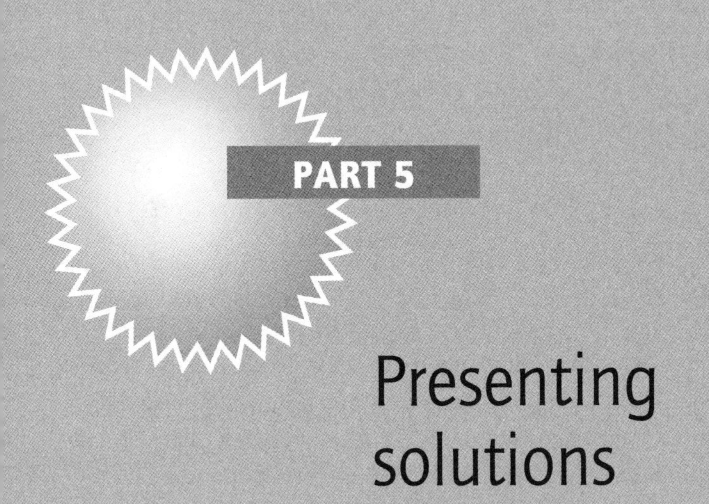

PART 5

Presenting solutions

I still remember my first day as a salesman. I was well prepared. I had undergone six weeks of rigorous training and I was pretty watertight on many of the key product lines. I had my new car, clean and polished. My case was full and neat. My shoes were shiny, my suit was pressed and my shirt was ironed. I was a man on a mission – ready for action! And so I went to talk to buyers and prospects – lots of them. And I told them all about our fabulous product range. No one bought from me on that first day, even though I presented (I thought) wonderfully! After a week, only a handful had bought. I was worried. My area manager was due to come out with me. I was even more worried. Once he had spent a morning with me, his feedback was straight to the point: 'Your product knowledge is great – you know your stuff. But you are not relating it to the customers. Sell solutions, not products.' Good advice then, still good advice now.

So that is what this part is all about – presenting solutions to customers and prospects. You might be selling complex solutions, everyday FMCG (fast-moving consumer goods) deals, two-minute pitches on the telephone, or part of a procurement process that can take weeks and endless bits of paper. Whatever your situation, there will be areas of interest that will help you improve the way you present a solution to customers so that it is compelling, persuasive and focused on them!

This section will focus on how to persuade with conviction and clarity. It will answer some important questions:

- How do you use benefit selling that does not sound contrived?
- How do you identify what to focus on when you sell?
- What should be included in a written proposal?
- How do you prepare effectively for a formal sales presentation?
- What does a persuasive delivery look like, sound like and feel like?
- How do you handle a genuine objection effectively?
- What has closing got to do with modern selling?

Appealing to the customer

There has been a lot written about features and benefits in selling. The intention here is to cut through the fluff and focus on what really matters when it comes to positioning a product or service. Taking the time to communicate clearly the benefits to your target market will provide a message that will resonate with your buyers, leading to increased sales of your product or service.

> *'The future lies in designing and* ***selling*** *computers that people don't realise are computers at all.'* – Adam Osbourne, US entrepreneur and pioneer of portable computing

Let us be clear about some distinctions immediately:

brilliant definitions

A **feature** is any characteristic of a product or service that remains the same whether the prospect or customer buys or not. These characteristics can include size, quality, payment terms, specialisation, technical details, factory location, product specifications (including size, weight, or colour) or anything else to do with describing the details of your product/service or company.

An **advantage** is the performance characteristic of a service that describes how it can be used or will help the customer. Advantages are what some features provide. Examples of advantages are a photocopier that copies two sides of a page at once, or a coffee shop that offers wireless internet access.

Benefits are the favourable results that the buyer receives from the service/product because of a particular advantage that has the ability to satisfy a customer's need/want. Benefits are statements that explicitly demonstrate how your service/product meets the needs of a customer. A benefit describes the individual value the advantage has for this particular customer as defined by their unique goals and priorities.

A **USP** – unique selling proposition – is something you or your company has that no other company has.

A **key differentiator** is a feature that is better than the main competitor in some way(s).

brilliant example 1

Feature: Power steering

Advantage: Fluid is pumped into a cylinder that helps make the wheels turn with less effort.

Benefit: Makes parking easier – reduces the time it takes to get into a tight space.

brilliant example 2

Feature: Wrist-watch

Advantage: Tells you the time accurately.

Benefit: Ensures you are not late to important appointments.

Think about it – what is important here is the benefit, not the advantage or feature. Too often we promote features when it is benefits that our customers are buying. We buy petrol to go places not because of the value of the liquid itself. Nobody who bought a drill wanted a drill. They wanted a hole. Here's a revelation: skydivers don't need parachutes. What they need is what the parachute does for them. Specifically, they need a tool to slow themselves down before they hit the ground. If there were a better way to soften the impact than a parachute, the parachute's days might be numbered. Think about what has happened to the typewriter, or the slide rule.

Although we sometimes seem to get attached to certain products it is, after all, the benefits of the product that we seek; not, generally, the features or the advantages. We are not saying that features are not important. Some buyers will have a genuine interest in them and so you should not simply gloss over them. As ever, pay attention to what interests the buyer.

In sales, we do well to realise that typically people buy benefits, not features or advantages. Whether you are in B2B sales, B2C sales, internet sales, retail sales, or you are selling professional services, benefits are what sell your product or service. The trick is to orientate your presentations and sales conversations, either face to face or on the telephone, so that you present **selective** benefits – not features – to the customer. Because buyers are now more sophisticated they will get turned off by poor use of the feature–benefit model, which was born out of the transactional method of selling.

people buy benefits, not features or advantages

Selling benefits

You can help yourself to differentiate between features and benefits, as you develop sales presentations, by stating a feature and then linking that with a benefit using the words 'which means' and/or 'so that'. For example: Power steering helps make the wheels turn with less effort, *which means that* it makes parking easier and reduces the time it takes to get into a tight space.

The focus of your communication should be on how your product/service can solve, address, improve, or reduce any area of difficulty that the specific customer/prospect outlines. When you consider the benefits that you will be articulating to the buyer, it is helpful to ask these sorts of questions:

- How will my product or service solve a problem for the customer?
- How will my service fulfil a client's want/need?
- In what way is my product better than the competition's?
- How does my price compare?
- Will my service improve the customer's life? Make them happier? Reduce risk? Make them more productive? Reduce costs in the long run?
- Does my product last longer than the competition's?

The key point here can be positioned in one sentence:

Most buyers will buy because of the benefits to them of your product/service (and because a problem is being solved), not the specific features that are part of the product/service.

If you really think about it, you can link most benefits at the highest level to:

- **Money**: the product or service helps the buyer make or save money and so improves competitiveness.
- **Time**: the product or service helps the buyer save time or frees up time for doing other things and so increases efficiency.
- **Ego**: the product or service in some way makes the buyer feel good or increases work/life balance.

But forget about selling generic benefits. The knack in representing benefits is to focus on the specific problems and issues of the customer in front of you. Make all benefits customer-focused.

> make all benefits customer-focused

You will lack credibility if you focus just on generic benefits. Specific benefits must be supported by features. A benefit statement, such as 'Our new software will improve productivity by as much as 20 per cent, saving you £29,000 per year and paying for itself within 14 months', must be accompanied by the features that bring about those benefits or your target market won't believe the benefits – they will have no credibility.

Focusing on the customer

Many salespeople fall into the trap of spending too much time on selling features. I wanted to buy a flat-screen TV just after Christmas. I went into a high-street shop and the salesperson started talking to me about pixels, colour decoding infrared commands and compatible HDMI devices. What was important to me was that it went on the wall nicely, that the picture quality was good and that it would be child-friendly. I was not asked what I wanted, however. I had to stop him after a few minutes and tell him!

So he got a second chance and I did buy a TV, but you may not get a second chance to present a solution, so you need to know the most effective ways of delivering persuasive information. Buyers always buy to move away from problems or something that creates pain (in this case, the large space that my TV took up in the lounge) and/or towards pleasure (in this case a much-improved picture and HD-ready). They always buy to solve specific problems.

I have seen business experts from major organisations include the following kinds of information in sales presentations:

- When their business was established.
- How many offices they have.
- Multiple service offerings.
- Organisation of the sales force.

None of these is particularly relevant unless it is linked with the buyer's interests/problems.

Most products or services have many features that could be attractive to a buyer. The trick is to align what you say with the interests of the prospect/buyer. The importance of benefits will change, dependent on the target audience. In many cases, a variety of decision makers (and influencers) are involved in a purchasing decision. You must tailor your promotional materials and your sales presentation to each one.

align what you say with the interests of the prospect/buyer

In many sales situations you know who you are competing against. One step to take before deciding your sales focus is to identify what areas are likely to be of most interest to the buyer. You can do this by completing this table:

USPs vs. the competitor	Key differentiators	Same as	Worse than

Basically, you will be focusing your sales efforts on the USPs (if you can think of any) and the key differentiators. The reality is that because of fierce competition it may be that you can find no USPs – so you need to focus on your key differentiators, from the point of view of the customer.

The 'same as' and 'worse than' features are likely to be some of the objections you may face.

brilliant exercise

Go ahead and try this out.

1. Specifically identify a customer group to which you want to communicate.
2. Describe your product or service in 25 words or less.
3. List the problems your product or service solves for the above customer group and/or the needs and wants the product or service meets for the group.
4. With the above information in mind, complete the table below.
5. Test each feature and benefit statement using the 'So what?' test. One of the difficulties in crafting your own feature and benefit statements is that the benefits of a particular feature are so clear to you that you assume they are evident to your target market as well. A dangerous assumption! If it is really not persuasive then eliminate it from the sales presentation.

You will now have the basics of how to position your product or service.

Compared to the competition, here is how you stack up:

USPs vs. the competitor	Key differentiators	Same as	Worse than

brilliant recap

This chapter has been about how we position what we want to sell. So here, in summary, are the key points to remember:

- Many buyers are just not interested in features in isolation.
- There is a distinction between features, advantages and benefits, and Brilliant Salespeople know how and in what sequence to articulate the distinctions.
- Buyers buy benefits that solve specific problems.
- Choose benefits that differentiate your product or service from the competition – if you have real USPs, then tell buyers!

For some of you, positioning your product or service is done in a face to face meeting or over the telephone. However, for many a written proposal of some sort is needed. Unless we know how to do this effectively we may reduce our chance of success by not answering the prospect's needs.

CHAPTER 21

Writing great sales proposals

Winning business in today's highly competitive market often means you will have to write some type of proposal. Whether you are trying to win a new customer or sell an idea to a current customer, your sales proposal is unlikely to win you the deal but it could easily lose you the deal.

'Few writers think of the messages they are trying to communicate in a report.' – Bruce Ross-Larson, *Riveting Reports*

Getting results

Your proposal is a sales, not a technical, document. It is imperative that you demonstrate your credibility, understanding and customer focus in every proposal that you present to your customer or prospect. What can you do to produce a high-quality sales document that gets results? Just follow these ten commandments to get you to the promised land!

demonstrate your credibility, understanding and customer focus in every proposal

1 Elicit criteria for the proposal

When you are with your prospect/buyer, and you have got to the point when it has been agreed that you should write a proposal, spend some time identifying what the decision maker would like to see in the proposal. Avoid assumptions. Simply ask questions such as:

- What would you like to see in this proposal?
- What will a really good proposal look like for you?
- What annoys you in proposals?
- Who is going to be reading this document?
- Are you a big-picture or detail person?

Once you have elicited the criteria, summarise and then confirm this by email. You are getting lots of yes's before anything has been written and demonstrating that you are customer-focused.

2 Under-promise and over-deliver

Think carefully before you commit to getting the proposal back to the buyer by a certain date. Most proposals do not have to be written yesterday, however pressing the requirement. You know how annoying it is when you are on a train that has stopped and the conductor informs you that you will be leaving in just a few minutes. If you are stuck there 20 minutes later it feels even worse – so avoid this trap. It is best to pick a date that is realistic and then complete it ahead of time. In this way you are under-promising and over-delivering. Customers love this.

3 Make sure proposals are customer-focused

When you start writing the proposal, ensure that you focus on the customer. Customers need to know that they have been heard and understood. Customers expect you to be responsive to the requirements that they have outlined, whether those requirements were provided verbally or documented in a formal Request For Proposal (RFP). If the prospective client has sent you an RFP, read it assiduously. Most RFPs include specific guidelines regarding submitting your sales proposal – so, do what you are told!

Use their language – identify their concerns, and their challenges. Focus on matching any proposal with a need or want that has been identified in the needs analysis selling phase. Cite your customer's name throughout the proposal. I always note specific words down when I am making notes during an initial meeting – and then play these hot buttons back to the buyer in the proposal. It demonstrates that you were listening and that you can empathise!

4 Brainstorm

Whether you write the proposal in isolation or as part of a team, spend some time brainstorming. Identify lots of things you could include and then start paring them down to manageable chunks of information. Here are the sorts of questions that will get your creative juices flowing:

- What is the customer's core issue?
- Why is this problem so important?
- What does the customer want?
- What are the measurement criteria?
- What options does the customer have?
- What is our value proposition?
- How can we prove that it will work?

Once the brainstorming is over you can start outlining your proposal and preparing a rough draft.

5 Use a template

Create a basic template that you can adapt for each proposal. It will save you time. A typical proposal will include:

- Executive summary.
- Introduction.
- Identification of issues/challenges.
- Alternatives.
- Recommendation.
- Process – show the steps to provide whatever it is your potential client needs.
- Investment required.
- Summary.

For more information about proposal templates see **www.brilliant-selling.com**.

6 Write well

We all have different styles, but here are some basics to bear in mind. Use these guidelines to make your proposal easy to read and evaluate:

- Use section headings to help the reader understand the logic of your proposal.
- Avoid confusing sentence structures – keep sentences short and coherent.
- Avoid using words, expressions or three-letter acronyms that will not be readily understood by the reader.
- Use 10–12 point font size.
- Limit paragraph length. Lengthy paragraphs appear text-heavy, so restrict your paragraphs to 10 lines.
- Break up the text with some visuals and graphics. Effective proposal graphics can include charts, photographs, cartoons, graphs and diagrams.
- Use a spell checker.

7 Substantiate all claims you make in your proposal

Buyers will be on the lookout for over-exaggerated claims. Ensure you can back up what you are saying. Use real-life examples and case studies and illustrate how your organisation differs from and is better than the competition.

> buyers will be on the lookout for over-exaggerated claims

8 Offer alternatives

We often position our proposals as discussion documents, and they can seem too formal and restrictive. Identify a number of alternatives and your buyer will then feel as though they have more choice. Your proposal should, ideally, include all alternatives – including what the competition is or may be offering and the consequences of doing nothing. Frequently proposals are done too quickly and are too limited in scope. Ensure there is room for creativity and input from the customer.

9 Write a strong executive summary

An executive summary is often the last thing you write but the first thing that the customer reads. It provides a consolidated summary of all the key points that are included in your proposal.

Let's be realistic. Many buyers, and especially others involved in the decision-making process, will simply choose not to read your entire document. So ensure your executive summary is accurate, interesting and persuasive – avoid grovelling or profusely thanking the buyer for the opportunity. Customers should never have to search for your key responses.

10 Follow up and present if you can

Ideally you want to present the proposal at the same time as you deliver it. This may not always be practical. If you are unable to present formally, send a hard and soft copy of your proposal and make sure it looks great. Telephone soon afterwards for feedback.

If you are able to present aspects of the proposal formally, your chances of winning the work are immediately strengthened because you can answer queries and back up your recommended solutions with additional information.

brilliant recap

Your sales proposal will not win you the deal but it could lose you the deal. However, it will *help* you to win the deal if you remember the ten commandments of great proposal writing:

1. Elicit criteria for the proposal.
2. Under-promise and over-deliver.
3. Make sure proposals are customer-focused.
4. Brainstorm.
5. Use a template.
6. Write well.
7. Substantiate all claims you make in your proposal.
8. Offer alternatives.
9. Write a strong executive summary.
10. Follow up and present if you can.

If you are able to present, the next section will provide you with some ideas about how to make a real impact when making sales presentations.

Preparing winning pitches

Sales presentations can come in many different guises. Here are some contrasting ways in which people pitch for business:

- Formal or informal.
- Individual or as a team.
- In front of one or a few people, or in front of many people.
- Long or short.
- With questions or without questions.
- With visual aids or without visual aids.

How do you present now? There are many great books about presenting so we want to focus specifically on sales presentations. Whatever way you and your company present, this is where you really earn your money. This is the performance element – get this wrong and you can be out of the door swiftly. Get it right and your presentation can be the differentiator that wins you the business. As with so many aspects of sales, it all starts with the preparation …

How to write a great sales presentation for a formal pitch

> *'Men stumble upon the truth from time to time, but most pick themselves up and hurry off as if nothing has happened.'* – Winston Churchill, British statesman

This section is aimed at salespeople who have to deliver a formal pitch, perhaps on the back of a proposal. There is a six-step process to effective preparation for a sales presentation. So let us look at each step in some detail.

1 Identify your outcome

> identify the reason why you are speaking

Your first step in preparation is to identify the reason why you are speaking and what you hope to achieve. It is critical that you have a specific objective for the presentation. This may not always be 'to come away with an order' but may include 'gaining agreement to meet the main decision maker', or 'ensure that the main decision maker understands our USP and how this benefits their business', or something else. Decide how you want your audience to feel, to think, and what action you want them to take as a result of your presentation.

Identify the positive audience reaction that you want, e.g. 'By the end of my presentation I want them to have confidence in my new proposals and be eager to start implementing them.'

What do you want them to take away from your presentation? If there is one core message, what is it?

2 Research your audience

> find out as much as possible about your audience

You need to find out as much as possible about your audience before you begin your preparation. For example:

- Why are they there? What are they expecting? What are their wants and needs?
- How much do they know about the subject?

- How much do they need to know so that you will achieve your objective?
- What is their attitude likely to be to you and your organisation?
- Have they any past experience that will influence them towards or against you?
- Are decision makers present?
- Will they read your proposal beforehand?

You need to plan your whole presentation from the point of view of your audience. Only include material that will be of interest, benefit or concern to them. Use examples that they can relate to. Ask yourself, 'If I were in their shoes, what would I want to hear?'.

'If I were in their shoes, what would I want to hear?'

Researching your audience will also enable you to establish a connection with them at the start of your sales presentation by showing that you understand their problems and concerns.

brilliant tip

Wherever possible, and when appropriate, always try to contact the individuals you will be presenting to in advance. This enables you to build some rapport before you present to them.

The key point here is that all sales presentations should be audience-centric rather than you-centric.

3 Brainstorm

You may or may not be part of the creative element of putting a presentation together. There may be a temptation to 'cobble' a sales presentation together using previous presentations and only making small adjustments. Avoid this mistake!

If you are part of the team, or if you are producing a presentation yourself, you can't be creative and organised at the same time – ideas don't come in order, so use an 'ideas map' to brainstorm your topic as follows:

- Write the subject of your presentation in a circle in the centre of a large sheet of paper.
- Write down all the ideas and thoughts you have on the subject, starting from the circle and branching out along lines of connecting ideas. Ideally use different-coloured pens.
- Let your mind be as free as possible. Do not restrict your thoughts by deciding where each point should go in a list. Your ideas should flow easily.
- When you have finished, link any related ideas and sections.
- Now you are ready to select the appropriate information to include in your presentation.

4 Select and structure your material

When you have completed your ideas map, you will almost certainly have more material than you require to deliver a great sales presentation. Now start selecting suitable information against your specific objective, your audience's needs and expectations and the time available. Avoid going straight to creating a slideshow. Include the key elements from a sales proposal, if you have had to write one.

A mistake in a pitch is to think you have to tell them everything about you and your organisation. Audiences are generally interested in what you can do for them! So go for a simple structure that focuses on the audience's interests.

Nobody can remember a great mass of detail – and they almost certainly don't need to, either. If you give people too many facts you overload them, and they end up remembering nothing. So, concentrate on a few key facts. Ask yourself 'If my audience goes away remembering only three or four key facts, which ones should they be? What is critical for them to know so that they can make a judgement about our suitability?'.

You need to find examples and anecdotes to illustrate your key facts and bring your presentation alive. Many presentations fail because they are over-dependent on facts and lack imaginative word-pictures.

Your presentation must have a logical structure. There are many possibilities – for example, a chronological sequence, or points in the order of importance, or showing the problem followed by the solution, or an explanation of theory followed by a demonstration of how it works in practice. Select the best structure for your objective and audience. It will help you if you give each section and sub-section a clear and specific heading. We tend to use a formula created by Bernice McCarthy in the USA in the 1970s, called the 4MAT system. The idea is that you break your presentation into specific sections, each one reflecting different preferences that will be there in the audience – **why, what, how, what if**.

- **Why** is this important to the audience? Get them motivated to listen. Cover the why at the beginning of your sales presentation.
- **What** – the audience needs information. Ideally, restrict your sales information to three key salient areas.
- **How** is it going to work? You might demonstrate how a system or product works, or the process that follows a purchase.
- **What if** – for those who wish to explore the future consequences of buying your product/service. What sort of impact is it going to have on the business?

The 4MAT system is practical, easy to understand and easy to utilise in sales presentations.

Only start thinking about your visual aids when you know what you are going to say; don't plan your presentation around them.

5 Focus on the start and the finish

The start and finish of a presentation are critical, because of the primacy and recency effect – people tend to remember more easily what they witnessed first and last.

The start must be punchy, attention-getting and capture the audience immediately. It tells people why they should listen, what you are going to talk about and the scope of your presentation.

Here is what you need to cover:

- An introduction to you (if some or all in the audience do not know you).
- The length of time the presentation will last.
- When you intend to take questions.

brilliant tip

The COMB structure can help you structure your presentation effectively. Make sure you cover each element of it:

C = Context – relevance to the audience.

O = Objective – the goal of the presentation.

M = Map – the agenda that you will follow.

B = Benefits – the *why*: what's in it for them? What will they get as a result of listening carefully?

The conclusion should be short, definite and conclusive. Summarise the main points and, if appropriate, state the next action.

6 Practise

Always rehearse a sales presentation. Stand up, and do it for real. Do not keep going back to the beginning each time you stop – otherwise you may never rehearse the ending! Remember to time the whole talk, and aim to finish it a few minutes short of your time slot. Practise as a team, if appropriate, or in front of colleagues, and, when possible, practise in the same room in which you are delivering the presentation.

brilliant recap

This six-step process is ideal as a process to follow when you are delivering a formal pitch. It will allow your sales presentation to be focused, creative and centred on the audience.

1. Identify your outcome.
2. Research your audience.
3. Brainstorm.
4. Select and structure your material.
5. Focus on the start and the finish.
6. Practise.

Once you have practised and made changes as appropriate, then you are ready to deliver the sales presentation. For a more detailed list of what to do before any sales presentation, please visit **www.brilliant-selling.com**.

An important part of many pitches is the effectiveness of the presentation that you make. You need to be able to deliver your message in a persuasive way. Want to find out more about how to do that easily? Then read on to the next chapter ...

Persuasive delivery

We have all been subjected to boring or feature-heavy sales presentations, either face to face or on the telephone. They put us off buying. The key to a formal sales presentation is to really engage the audience – bored buyers do not buy. If you engage them, you stand a chance! In order to really engage any audience when you are delivering a formal sales pitch there are four areas that, if done well, will put you in the pantheon of great presenters:

bored buyers do not buy

- Strong and open body language.
- Visual aids that help the audience.
- Presenters that look like a team.
- Presentations that hook the audience.

'To convert somebody go and take them by the hand and guide them.' – St Thomas Aquinas, Italian philosopher and theologian

Body language

Strong and open body language will support the content of any sales presentation. Here is how you do it:

- Get grounded by ensuring your feet are shoulder-width apart and facing the audience. Stand tall and you will be perceived as a confident person. Undirected movement of the legs and feet shows that you are nervous and feel uncomfortable in front of the audience. Swaying, rocking, standing on one foot and even little dances all reveal your inner anxiety. Learn to stand still and direct your energy to your audience.

- Allow your hands to fall to the side or clasp them gently over your stomach. This is the most neutral resting position.
- Retain eye contact with the audience throughout – not like a scared rabbit that has to check all the escape routes, but in a calm and interested manner as you would when talking to a good friend. Avoid looking at:
  - visual aids
  - the floor or ceiling
  - your notes
  - the most senior person present
  - the friendliest person present
  - or even out of the window.
- In a formal sales presentation, always stand, if possible, as it will give you more authority, more breath and therefore a stronger voice, but above all it will give you the flexibility to move around and stay in control. Avoid the following:
  - Fiddling with rings, watches, cuff-links, paper clips, glasses, coins in pockets or elastic bands.
  - Touching and patting hair, face, pockets, desk or table.
- Your gestures should coincide with what you are saying and naturally add emphasis to your words. Remember that gestures should include the whole of your arm and not be restricted to small, meaningless hand movements.
- Smile. It will make the audience want to listen to you instead of being discouraged by a hostile glare.

Ensure your visual aids are visual and aid the audience!

Avoid a slow death from a thousand slides. Too many people use too many slides during a presentation and basically bore the pants off people!

Many visual aids fail because they are not visual. They should be used to help the audience, and not as a prompt for the speaker. If you think part of your presentation may be boring without visual aids, work on making the **content** more interesting.

There are many visual aids available to you – story boards, products, posters, white boards, as well as PowerPoint. Did you know that Microsoft estimates that there are considerably more than 30,000,000 PowerPoint presentations made *every* day? You are never going to differentiate yourself by using PowerPoint alone. Be creative, especially in pitches for new business. Here is a real chance to be distinctive and show why you are the best choice!

All visual aids should be simple, clear and visual. Their purpose is to help the audience, not to remind you of what you want to say.

all visual aids should be simple, clear and visual

Good visual aids can:

- Show the relationship or comparison between data (bar chart or pie chart).
- Build up a picture.
- Illustrate a process.
- Summarise key points.

Successful visual aids have:

- Bold, contrasting colour.
- Consistency – the same background colour throughout and a uniform typeface.

- Simplicity – one idea per slide.
- Good design – so the eye moves to the essential elements.

What to avoid when designing visual aids:

- Reproduction of computer printouts.
- Tables of figures.
- Complex diagrams.
- Reproduction of forms.
- Excessive words (maximum of seven words per line and five lines if using bullet points).

Before your presentation:

- Think carefully about where you are going to stand – don't block the screen.
- Make sure you know how to operate the equipment.
- Have all your visual aids in order, numbered clearly.
- Take a back-up copy on a memory stick.

During your presentation:

- Do not show the visual aids until you are ready to talk about them.
- Introduce the whole visual before you start to talk about the detail.
- Give people time to look at them – don't whisk them off at top speed.
- Avoid talking to the visual aids. Remember, there are *people* out there who want to hear you!
- Resist the urge to repeat the words displayed in your bullet points – remember, most of your audience will also be able to read! Add value to one or two points on the slides with what you say.

Delivering sales presentations as a team

> there are sound reasons why a team approach can work well

You may choose to present in teams when winning new business or retaining existing business. There are specific areas to focus on when you are presenting as a team, which are fundamental to the success of the presentation. There are sound reasons why a team approach can work well.

When we work with salespeople who present in teams and have been unsuccessful in winning a piece of business there are some common themes that emerge from the feedback they receive from customers:

- 'They presented more as a group of individuals rather than a single, cohesive team.'
- 'They seemed uncertain as to who had responsibility for each section of the presentation.'
- 'They were not consistent in how they presented or in the quality of the presentation.'

Often, the team that presents to win some business does not operate each day as a team, so there is likely to be some lack of familiarity between individuals. For a team presentation to be effective, you must practise together and pay attention to how you work as a team.

Here are some important tips on presenting as part of a team:

- Decide the key goal of the presentation and make sure that everyone presenting understands it.
- As you are planning your presentation, make sure that you keep everyone in the loop in terms of amendments, changes in attendees or timings, etc. Make sure that no one is 'surprised' by anything on the day.
- Decide on who should be present based on what the customer/prospect needs. Everyone in the presenting team should add value.

- Make sure that everyone understands their specific role in the presentation. This is especially pertinent if you are asking someone senior to present as part of your team.
- Make sure that you play to your strengths. Not everyone needs to present. It may be, for example, that you have a 'technical expert' there for questions even if they are not formally presenting.
- Make sure you rehearse together as a team. As part of rehearsing, it is important to:
  - Give each other specific, objective feedback on what they do well and what could be improved.
  - Rehearse the whole presentation from start to finish.
  - Agree and rehearse the handovers from one person to another (this is one area where a team can come across as uncoordinated!).
  - Agree on who will handle questions, and practise taking and answering some of the more challenging potential questions.
- During the presentation, support each other with positive body language: good eye contact, nodding, etc.

brilliant tip

Email us at **resources@brilliant-selling.com** for a checklist on preparing for team presentations.

Final tips on how to engage the audience

'They may forget what you said, but they will never forget how you made them feel.' – Carl W. Buechner, US Presbyterian minister

The key thing with delivering a sales presentation is to engage the audience. Then they will really feel part of the presentation. Here are some final tips on how to do this:

- **Get into a resourceful, confident state**. To find out how to do this, take a look at Part 3 – Your power to influence.
- **Use sales materials wisely and sparingly**. Used well, these will give your presentation more credibility and will probably be used during the **how** stage.
- **Use multiple senses**. Your audience will get distracted (however outstanding you are as a presenter). You need to find ways of getting them interested and holding their attention. One way of doing this is to engage as many senses as possible in a presentation. We see, hear, feel (external touch and internal emotion), taste and smell. Include as many of these senses as possible in your presentation. Here are some suggestions:
  - Have music playing – especially at the beginning and end of your presentation. It will engage the audience and help get them or keep them in the desired state.
  - Ensure that there is visual stimulation. You may well be using a software package such as PowerPoint, but also consider playing a video, putting banners/posters up around the room, using a flipchart or drawing a picture.
- **Get your audience to do something**. Perhaps ask them to introduce themselves, explain their goals or answer a question. Involve them as much as you can.
- **Words are important**. Most people at your presentations are interested in what you have to say, so you want to ensure that your words are working for you and not getting lost. Use language that covers the three main senses – **visual, auditory** and **kinesthetic**:

  - **Visual**: see, look, picture, outlook, insight, reflect, glimpse, snapshot, brilliant, bright, colourful, illuminating.
  - **Auditory**: hear, listen, sound, say, tune in, dialogue, ring, chime, quiet, tell, echo, announce.
  - **Kinesthetic**: feel, grab, pull, grasp, get hold of, handle, tough, sharp, dig, impact.
- **Use your voice effectively**. Make sure that you vary your voice tone so that it is interesting to your audience and makes them want to listen. Some presenters we have heard have quite monotone voices that do not, necessarily, inspire interest. Be aware of your volume and speed of delivery (you may need to slow down, for example). See Part 3 for more information about delivering with rapport and credibility.

brilliant recap

In all formal buying situations that we have come across, part of the selection criteria is how you present your product/service. We have seen it make and break a deal and it is an area in which you can really engage your audience with a passionate presentation that reinforces what you have to offer. The four presentation elements we have focused on in this chapter are:

- Strong and open body language (get grounded, have a resting position, retain eye contact, stand, use supportive gestures and smile).
- Visual aids that help the audience (ensure they are audience-friendly, be creative, design them carefully use them with a light touch).
- Presenters that look like a team (have goals and roles and support each other).
- Presentations that hook the audience (use sales materials wisely, use multiple senses and get your audience involved).

Even with the best sales presentations, there are likely to be objections that crop up. These need to be respected and handled well.

Making the most of objections

In traditional sales training, salespeople are often taught to 'overcome' an objection. If you were buying, would you really like your objection 'overcome'? You would surely feel more comfortable if any objection was handled sensitively and addressed sensibly.

An objection is a reservation, or concern, about some aspect of a service/product that may prevent a sale taking place. The old adage here is correct – objections can be buying signals. They suggest that there is interest. Stony silence or a definite no indicates you have less chance of completing the sale! Objections may just be the buyer suggesting:

- 'Give me more information before I decide.'
- 'I need a little more proof that your product really will fill my needs.'
- 'I'm almost convinced, but I need just one more reason to justify me saying yes.'

Your task is to understand the reason for the concern and help provide a response that meets the concern.

> *'Nothing will ever be attempted if all possible objections must first be overcome.'* – Samuel Johnson, English author and lexicographer

brilliant exercise

What sort of objections do your buyers voice? Think about this question and list the most common objections that you encounter.

Typical objections involve:

- Price.
- Resistance to move to a new supplier (resistance to change is often a key motivator for objections).
- Concerns about some aspect of the product/service.
- Support offered.
- Timing (as in 'Let me think about it').

Begin with the right attitude. A salesperson must never appear nervous or hesitant when an objection is raised. Hesitating or diverting the eyes loses trust. To remain calm, remember that objections are opportunities to learn more about the client's needs. Top salespeople understand this and are eager to discuss whatever issue a client raises.

objections are opportunities to learn more about the client's needs

Often the best way to handle objections is to get them on the table at the beginning of your presentation or address them directly in your proposal. As in:

'I would imagine there are certain areas in which it would be important for you to gain some clarity ... I will address these directly during my presentation.'

Whatever the reason for an objection, the customer is, in effect, saying ...

I am not yet totally convinced that your solution addresses my needs ...

The 4A model

So here is a four-step process for handling objections successfully. It is known as the 4A model:

Acknowledge

Audience

Answer

Ask

Acknowledge

First, acknowledge the person who has made the objection: 'Thanks for raising this – I can understand why this is an important area for you.'

Audience

Then throw it open, if appropriate, to the audience if there is more than one person. Ask some questions to get clarity and give you a bit of time to think:

- 'On a scale of 1–10 how important is this?'
- 'Does everyone else share this concern?'

If there is life without your product or service, then there is life with your product or service. The prospect will experience one of these two scenarios ... guaranteed. The question is, do they see enough difference between them to make a choice that is different from the status quo? So one way of handling an objection is to be very upfront and paint a picture of what it will be like both with and without your product/service. Just ensure that life with your product/service looks a lot rosier!

The only person who can really 'deal' with an objection is the buyer/prospect. Until the prospect handles the objection in their own mind, it is not handled. So what does the prospect need to do to go inside themselves and handle the objection in a way that allows the sale to proceed? Saying 'Trust me, I'm a salesperson' is unlikely to work unless there is an extraordinary level of trust already built. What information do the prospects need in order for *them* to handle *their* objection? Think of objection-handling as facilitating a process within the prospect, rather than directing a process at the customer.

think of objection-handling as facilitating a process within the prospect

brilliant exercise

Take the objections you identified in the last exercise and identify what questions you can ask a buyer to facilitate their thinking:

Typical objection	Questions to ask

Answer

Now you have to address the issue. Avoid waffling, focus on making no more than three points and keep it simple and directly addressing the problem. Avoid becoming defensive by trotting out features – answer the objection by linking to the customer's needs and the selling value.

Ask

Ask the person who raised the objection if it has now been answered satisfactorily:

- 'How does that sound?'
- 'Has that addressed your concern?'
- 'Is there anything else you need to feel comfortable now?'

If the customer still has the concern then simply start at the first 'A' again and cycle through the process. It is sometimes possible, after you have completed the 4As process, to get commitment to buy the product/service there and then.

Price concerns

A common objection is often over price. This could, in fact, be a negotiation point. When faced with price concerns, probe:

- 'Before we talk about price, what other questions do you have about (insert your product/service)?'
- 'What is your main concern about price?'
- 'What do you need to know so that price is no longer an issue?'

Then sell the value of your product/service before addressing the price concern.

Handling objections

Here are ten final tips about handling objections:

1. Audience profiling should have helped you to anticipate objections and identify potential sources of difficulty in your 'pitch'.
2. Prepare for objections as thoroughly as for the main sales presentation.
3. Anticipate the three to five objections that you really *do not* want to be asked – especially for competitive pitches – and ensure you know how to handle them well.
4. Prepare support materials in anticipation of likely objections.
5. Get feedback during a sales pitch, as in 'So, what do you think?'. This will flush out some objections and avoid you getting a bunch of objections right at the end.
6. If you do not understand an objection, ask for clarity.
7. Avoid arguing with a buyer – listen carefully and respond with empathy and logic.
8. Listen not only to the words and their meaning but also to whatever emotional content is expressed in the objection.
9. If the questioner rambles and is unclear, summarise the objection to help the audience understand what point you are now addressing.
10. If you are presenting as part of a team, decide who is going to handle which objections. To ensure cohesion, you may choose to filter all objections through the leader of your team. Consider listing all objections on a flipchart before you handle them. This gives you time to think, and control over the order in which you answer them.

brilliant recap

Objections are likely to crop up in one form or another during a sale, and that's when you start earning your crust! The key points we want you to leave with are:

- Objections are often just buying signals in disguise.
- Anticipate objections and prepare how to answer them.
- Flush out any likely objections early.
- Avoid getting into a knockabout argument.
- Remain calm.
- Probe for more information.
- Answer the objection in a straightforward manner.
- Get agreement that the issue is sorted.

Objections do not have to be the stumbling blocks that they seem. Very quickly you can move towards commitment.

Closing and commitment

I still have the sales brochure for the first sales training I attended. The front cover proclaimed:

When I got to the location for the training, there were large posters with the same message and, underneath, '101 ways to get the buyer to say yes'. Wow! I was lost on about the 17th!

Up until the end of the 1980s there was a huge emphasis on closing as the magical, possibly mystical, element of selling. You will still find an enormous amount of material on the internet that will show how to close. Maybe you do have to get lots of people to say yes regularly: certainly any salesperson knows that there may be a point when they ask for the business. However, in this book this section will be one of the shortest. Why? Because people do not like to be 'closed'. Consumers, let alone professional buyers, are so much more savvy to 'closing techniques' and see them for the absurd attempts at manipulation that they are. We speak to many professional buyers and they lose respect for people who try to close before they are ready to buy.

Yes, of course customers still have to say yes, otherwise we would all be out of a job. And if you are working in a transactional environment, there may be more of a focus on closing. However, to generalise, buyers hate salespeople who use tired and outdated methods. So let us consign to the dustbin of history the Half Nelson, the Napoleon and any other type of close that is forced, transparent, manipulative and is likely to get you thrown out!

We prefer the word commitment. Throughout the sales process, you need to ensure there is momentum and commitment to the next stage – whether that be another meeting or the final decision. When assessing the outcome of a sales call, get clear on what is an advance and what is simply a stand-still result. Many people kid themselves that 'enhancing the relationship' means it was a good call. This is not an advance. No action or next step was agreed. Ask questions such as:

- 'Where do we go from here?'
- 'If you were in a position to work with us – when would a decision be made?'
- 'What do you want to focus on in the next meeting?'

Thinking of the 'close' as an act that happens at the end is simplistic and unrealistic. It happens throughout the process. A Brilliant Salesperson tests for commitment through all stages of the sale and will abandon the process if there is no real interest or commitment from the other party. Of course, you have to believe you can get the deal and that the deal is good for the prospect. What we are looking for here is a simple conclusion to a consultative process.

a Brilliant Salesperson tests for commitment through all stages of the sale

Focus on the relationship

Commitment at the end can be natural because if you have done your job right – identified needs and wants, matched these with specific benefits that your product/service brings and handled objections well – then there is a good chance the buyer will buy. Make the final approach natural – people don't like being sold to. Focus on the relationship, not the close.

Ask some anticipatory questions:

- 'What else do you need from us?'
- 'Do you have all the information required to make a decision?'
- 'Are we in a position to move towards discussing next steps?'

You may have to ask for commitment, but again make it simple:

- 'Are you happy to proceed now?'
- 'Have you heard enough for us to start working together?'
- 'What is the best way to move this forward now?'

> the final decision often happens without you in the room

The reality is that the final decision often happens without you in the room. That is fine. If you have done your job well, and think what you are offering is the best, you will get the business.

brilliant recap

In the final recap of this part of the book we want to remind you that:

- Traditional closing just does not work nowadays – buyers are too savvy and it is, frankly, clunky and mechanical. Avoid the worst type of end-game closing that had its day long ago!
- Customers still need to say yes, so you still need to get commitment.
- Test for commitment throughout the sales process – are they really interested?

Far from being an all-or-nothing, last-minute panic signal, getting commitment in a sale is a layered process that begins when a prospect agrees to meet you. Think of it in this way and that getting commitment is something that happens in business and in life all the time.

So, you have met any objections, gained commitment and made the sale. For a lot of you, the relationship doesn't end there. In fact, it is often just the beginning, if you are lucky. Part 6 looks at developing your customers.

PART 6

Developing customers

In the 1990s I had spent a significant amount of time developing a sales relationship with a prospect around a particular high-value product I was looking to sell. I had done everything 'by the book': I had met the decision makers and influencers, positioned the compelling benefits of our solution and our differentiator as a company and met their objections. Finally, I won the deal. It felt great, and off I went to manage the rest of my pipeline. Nine months later I was called by my customer to ask if I was interested in bidding for a new project. My customer was not sure if our software would be appropriate but wanted to give us a chance. I went in, full of confidence – our software did do what they wanted and the customer had a previous, positive experience of working with us. Imagine my frustration when I lost the opportunity to a major competitor. How could they? They knew we could deliver, they knew our service was great and I had a relationship with some of the main decision makers!

My lesson came when I visited my contact to get some feedback on why we had lost out. It was tough feedback to hear but it has stood me in good stead ever since. The successful competitor had done what I had done originally to get my first deal. They had taken time to meet with decision makers, they had listened to concerns, positioned specific elements of their solution that they found out were really important to the prospect and they had assumed nothing. I had made the critical mistake of believing that, just because I had invested time to understand the customer's needs around the initial opportunity, I could just pitch up and their loyalty to me would be enough to secure a project that I knew we were ideally suited for. I had assumed that, once I had secured the customer, I would naturally be at the front of their mind for future opportunities and, because of this belief, I simply focused on other prospects until the telephone rang.

Winning the initial sale is only part of the job of a Brilliant Salesperson. A relationship is not cultivated in a single sale. If you think about long-term relationships outside work, the real challenge once you have established them is to keep them!

In the final part of this book we will answer the following questions:

- Why is managing your existing customers a great use of your time?
- What are the key priorities in managing an existing customer?
- How can you develop a relationship that erects barriers to entry by competitors?
- What activities can you engage in to 'stack the cards' in favour of continued business from your customers?

The value of a customer

One of the things that the story in the introduction to this final part of the book really taught me was that you do not fully realise the value of having something until you lose it. Once I had secured the order, the customer took second place to the other deals I was working on and needed to close to make my numbers. Because of this, I lost focus on maintaining and developing the relationship and this led directly to me losing possible business.

you do not fully realise the value of having something until you lose it

There are a few things that are almost always true about a customer – someone we have sold something to at least once:

- They have invested in us as a salesperson. They have trusted us enough to buy from us.
- They have been sold on the value that we can bring them – at least around the original sale.
- They have taken us some time to develop – we have invested our time in them.
- In order to have influenced them to buy from us we probably had to build and demonstrate some level of rapport and credibility with them.

Both you and the customer have spent a lot of time and effort in getting to the point of making a sale. To some extent, there is already a positive relationship in place. But, like most relationships, if you do not invest a little time in maintaining and developing them, the quality begins to suffer and, when you next want to call on it, maybe the strength of relationship is not sufficient to give you the outcome you want. Maybe things have changed while you were busy on other things and other relationships.

> *'Treasure your relationships, not your possessions.'* – Anthony J. D'Angelo, US motivational speaker and educator

What is the cost of acquiring business?

Winning business has costs associated with it. We may not see a 'cash' value for the different steps involved but the cost is real enough. In economics there is a term called 'opportunity cost'. Simply defined, it means that putting our resources on one thing means you are foregoing using the same resource (time, for example) to achieve something else. For example, if you spend your hard-earned money on a car, that money is not now available as a deposit on a house. In sales terms, the question that it raises is: what could we have done with our time and what could it have yielded if we were not selling to this particular customer? We need to consider how much time and other resources we have spent securing this one customer in order to see the real value of our investment.

> work out the cost of acquiring the business in the first place

brilliant exercise

Take a few minutes to try and work out the cost of acquiring the business in the first place. While your sales situations may vary, consider the following table and make a guess at the time and monetary value (either for you or the company you work for) associated with each step listed:

	Time	Monetary value
Initial prospecting		
Meetings (including administration and follow-ups)		
Presentations and proposals		
Internal meetings and management of the prospect		
What is the value of missed opportunities that I could not focus on because I was spending time on this?		

While this table is not 'science', it can help us see how important it is to protect the investment we have made and maximise it through maintaining and developing the relationship.

brilliant tip

It is often five times easier to sell to an existing client than to generate a new client.

A well and proactively managed client is more likely to:

- Tell other people how pleased they are with your service levels, which may lead to new prospects.
- See you as a partner rather than a salesperson – someone not in it for a quick gain – which builds trust and loyalty, making it easier to identify and secure future sales.
- Erect barriers to entry for your competitors because of the strength of relationship that exists between you and the client.
- Take less time to sell products to in the future because they know you.

'A relationship, I think, is like a shark, you know? It has to constantly move forward or it dies. And I think what we got on our hands is a dead shark.' – Woody Allen, US film director

brilliant recap

Brilliant Salespeople understand the value of a customer. In this short chapter the key points that we have focused on are:

- It is five times easier to secure additional work from an existing client than to win a new client.
- There is a cost in acquiring a new client and, like any other investment we make, we should protect the investment and maximise its potential.
- We need to focus time on maintaining and developing the relationship with a customer or it will die!

If we truly understand the value of our customer over the longer term we are more likely to take the right steps to manage the relationship we have, and maximise the return on our investment in winning their business.

Managing the relationship

Having invested a lot of time in establishing a relationship with the customer that enables them to buy from us, it is important that we take time to maintain and develop the relationship if we have an interest in selling to this customer at some point in the future. For some of you, repeat purchases might represent a regular opportunity. For others, it may be that any repeat purchase is less frequent, possibly for a different product or service that you also sell (now or in the future) or for add-ons to the original sale.

Selling different products or services – possibly managed by other salespeople within your business – is called 'cross-selling' and it represents a real opportunity to extend the relationship with the customer and erect barriers to entry by a competitor by adding value in other areas of their business. Even if you are not responsible for the other product or service that can be sold, you can ask the customer questions to understand their need and make an introduction to the right person. This is likely to be reciprocated, so everyone wins in the long run.

Unless you have no real opportunity to sell to a customer again, managing the customer relationship is important. But how do you manage something as individual and subjective as a 'relationship'?

It is likely that a principle that works in many facets of life will also be true for you: 80 per cent of your business will come from 20 per cent of your customers. This Pareto Principle means we need to be clear and objective about which customers represent the real opportunity and ensure we spend adequate time developing those relationships.

> *'We control 50 per cent of a relationship. We influence 100 per cent of it.'* – Anon

What relationship do we want with our customer?

It is an interesting question to consider. We often do not think about defining a relationship in specific terms but, as you are likely to get more of what you focus on, we should consider what we want before we think about how we go about getting it!

---

brilliant exercise

1. Think of what an 'ideal' customer relationship would look like from **your** own perspective. Pick 5–10 words that would characterise the relationship.
2. Now put yourself **in the shoes of the customer**. From this perspective, what words would you use to describe the ideal relationship with your supplier?

To what extent do you take steps to create a relationship in line with your answer to the second question? To what extent do you think your own desired ideal relationship matches that of the customer's view?

If we think about sales relationships we have as a customer, we find that characteristics such as rapport, trust, adding value, honesty and so on are what are important to us. Any activities we engage in to manage customer relationships should, therefore, demonstrate and develop these traits. Alternatively, you could just ask the customer! Two great questions to find out where you need to focus your efforts are:

- 'What's important to you about your relationship with a supplier?'
- 'If I was doing a great job of managing our relationship with you, what would I be doing?'

Getting the relationship that you want

Clearly, the customer relationship is a commercial one and so it is appropriate for you to think about it in terms of what you want from it as well as from the customer's perspective.

If you are to be truly effective at managing customer relationships then you need to bear in mind the following five key points:

- Avoid making assumptions.
- Be proactive.
- Set relationship goals.
- Consider how you move the depth and value of the relationship forward.
- Consider how you manage difficulties when they occur.

Let us look in more detail at each of these points.

Avoid making assumptions

> *'Assumptions are the termites of relationships.'* – Henry Winkler, US actor and director

Salespeople often inflate the quality of the relationship they think they have with their customers. They like to think that their customers are going to be thinking about them whenever they have an opportunity to buy another product and that the relationship that exists will prevent competitors gaining entry to the account.

When you find yourself being a little complacent about the quality, depth or breadth of your customer relationship, challenge yourself to find evidence as to why your view of the relationship is correct. Typical areas where we can make assumptions that might prove incorrect and could damage the relationship, if not checked with the customer, include:

> 80 per cent of your business will come from 20 per cent of your customers

- How often to contact the customer to update them or just stay in touch.
- That the customer knows what else we do and how it could help them.
- That the customer will not meet with or consider products from competitors now that we have the relationship.
- That we have demonstrated, and continue to demonstrate, sufficient 'value add' for the customer to keep considering us.
- That their situation will stay the same over time.

Be proactive

Consider for a moment a successful long-term relationship that you have with someone outside or inside work. Do you occasionally pick up the phone to this person, think of them if you hear about something that might be of interest to them and pass it on, remember birthdays, or occasionally just do something because you know they will appreciate it?

Very few long-term relationships have survived without some effort. We need to work at them and that means being proactive. You see, relationship management is an important but not urgent task. It is one of those things that will not cause your business to fail tomorrow if you do not do it. But by the time it becomes urgent it will be too late.

If you think about your approach before you won the business and secured a client, you might characterise it as being 'hungry'. You demonstrated an interest and willingness to go the extra mile to secure a deal. You put effort in. Well, guess what, that is what your competitors are trying to do now with your customer!

Salespeople are sometimes characterised as either 'hunters' or 'farmers'. The hunters are those that live for the thrill of the sale. They like taking a prospect through to becoming a customer. They enjoy opening new accounts. The farmers enjoy cultivating the relationship. They are happy to sow seeds, knowing that they may take a while to come to anything. If repeat or additional sales to a customer are an opportunity, you need to be able to be a hunter and a farmer. Six years ago I won a small piece of work with the UK arm of an international corporation. I focused on doing a great job and on developing a relationship with the key decision maker. I would keep them informed of things that I thought would be of interest, I put them in touch with people where I thought there could be benefit for both parties. Last year this customer represented 10 per cent of our business.

Some examples of being proactive in managing a customer relationship include:

- Forwarding useful articles or information that you come across and think might be of value to them.
- Making introductions that might be beneficial to your customer.
- Checking how things are going with the product/service they bought from you.
- Seeking ways to develop additional contacts within the same customer.
- Meeting up less formally to find out what is current, what has changed and what the priorities are for your customer.

Set relationship goals

The only thing that is consistent about all relationships is that they are all different! No two customer relationships will be identical because they involve different personalities, cultures and situations. If you are to manage relationships effectively you need first to understand where you are now with this individual relationship and then define where you want it to be, specifically. You need to set relationship goals.

> you need to set relationship goals

The challenge here is that relationships are subjective things and goals need to be objective. The key to making relationship goals more objective is to look for evidence of success. An important question is 'When I have achieved this relationship goal, how will I know?' An example will help. Let us say that you wish to develop more trust. You first need to consider how you would know if the desired level of trust existed. It may be that your customer would introduce you to their manager so you can present how you can help the business in another area; they would give you information that would help position your proposal more effectively and they would act as a telephone reference for one of your prospects. If this is the evidence that you would see, you can then start to create an action plan that would help you achieve that goal.

brilliant exercise

Pick one of your customers and consider the relationship that exists. How would you like to develop the relationship?

Ask yourself how you would know when this relationship goal was achieved – how would the achievement be evidenced, either in terms of what you would see or what would happen as a result?

Set some goals based on achieving the 'evidence'. Make the goals specific and measurable and set a date for their achievement.

Goals do not need to be limited to the relationship itself, of course. You might well have tangible revenue goals for future business through this customer.

you might well have tangible revenue goals for future business through this customer

Consider how you move the depth and value of the relationship forward

Setting specific goals is important if you are to move the relationship forward, but it helps to have some context for these goals; some sense of the relationship 'journey' that you are looking to take your client on. If you can increase the depth of relationship you have with customers, you are erecting barriers for competitors and increasing your chances of additional sales going forward.

One model that is widely used is to consider different levels of relationship that exist. This can help you consider your priorities and the actions you need to take generically to help move customer relationships forward. Often, specific definitions depend on your company, context and customers, but the following provides an illustration of how this approach can work.

The start point is objectivity. You need to define the different relationship 'levels' that could exist and what, specifically, characterises them. You may have the following definitions:

Level	Definition
Prospect	Someone who has not yet bought from me but is a qualified potential customer.
Customer	Someone who has bought from me once. They may or may not have any loyalty to me.
Client	Someone who has bought from me more than once. They have demonstrated that they see the value I offer.

Supporter	Someone who acts as a reference for me. I have relationships with all the key decision makers and 70+ per cent of the influencers.
Advocate	I have a close relationship at senior management and middle management levels. I know all the decision makers and influencers. I share strategic plans and the customer inputs ideas and suggestions into my product development.

As you move from prospect to advocate you are increasing the depth and quality of the relationship that exists. This makes it far more difficult for competitors to get in the door.

Getting the relationship that you want!

brilliant exercise

Consider what levels of relationship would be appropriate and desirable in your context.

How would you define them?

Now classify your existing customers into these levels – be objective!

Defining relationship levels enables you to then ask such questions as: 'What do I need to do to move a client to a supporter?'. This will give rise to some specific actions that you can take.

For a case study and more information on how to use the relationship model, visit **www.brilliant-selling.com** and request the resource pack.

Consider how you manage difficulties when they occur

> *'Even the best of friends face conflicts, but that needn't mean the end of the relationship.'* – Anon

In most long-term relationships, problems or difficulties occur. It is just a fact of life and sales is no different. Difficulties come in many forms, big and small, and examples in sales include:

- Late delivery to your customer.
- Having a particularly aggressive negotiation over terms.
- Giving the customer incorrect information by mistake.
- Not following through on a commitment you made.

While we do what we can to avoid difficulties occurring, what separates Brilliant Salespeople from the rest is how they respond to and manage difficulties when they do, inevitably, arise. A difficulty can be defined as anything that can disrupt the relationship that we have. In itself, it could be a small thing, something that is not, on its own, enough to create a big problem. The issue is that if we ignore enough of the small things by brushing them under the carpet or giving a response to the customer that does not truly satisfy them, then the next 'small' thing could be the 'straw that breaks the camel's back'.

These small, individual difficulties are called 'pinches' and there is a well-documented model called, unsurprisingly, the Pinch model that describes what happens if we do not deal with individual pinches effectively. When we become aware of a pinch, the temptation might be to resolve it in the quickest way we can. So, for example, if we send out an incorrect invoice and our customer queries it we may be tempted simply to correct it and send out a new one. We feel that we have dealt with the issue – but think of it from the customer's perspective. They may feel that we have not taken the mistake seriously or that we did not appreciate how important it was for them. This might lead them to question other things we do and the quality of our relationship.

An incorrectly addressed pinch can lead to a perception by the customer that we are avoiding the real issue and this, in turn, can lead to mistrust. This means that the individual issues never really get resolved to the satisfaction of the customer. They simply build up on top of one another and can seriously damage the relationship, which could end in a 'crunch' time. The danger is that any one of these small difficulties might not seem too important to us and, indeed, in isolation it may not be. We need to manage difficulties proactively and in a timely way. Doing this will build a stronger, more trusting relationship.

we need to manage difficulties proactively and in a timely way

When we become aware of a possible pinch point we need to recognise this as something that might be important to the customer and then use it as a way of going back to them to a) let them know we are concerned and want to address the issue in the right way, and b) use it as an opportunity to make more explicit how we will work together going forward to avoid similar issues occurring. By making relationship expectations and 'ways of working' explicit in this way we build an understanding of how the relationship should work.

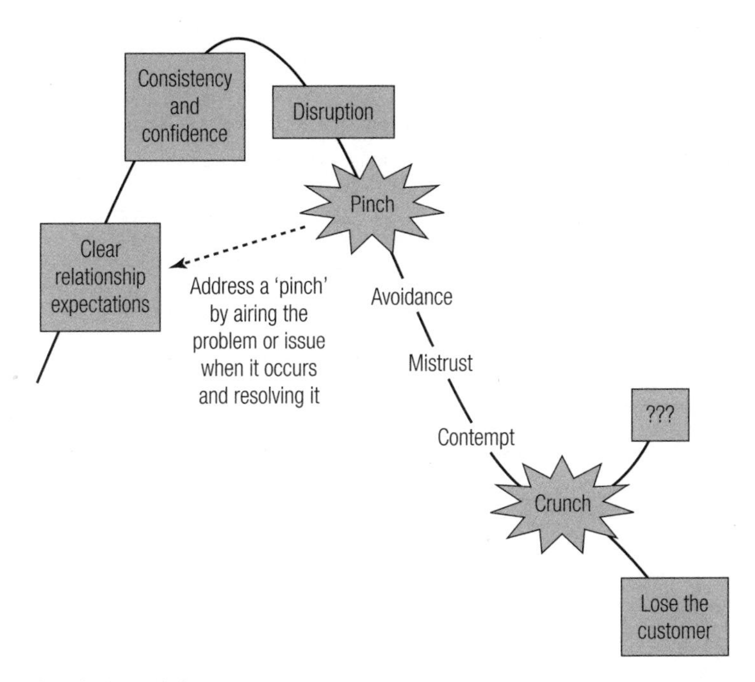

The Pinch model

One thing that can hold us back from 'having the difficult conversation' is that we do not know how to approach the conversation and we are fearful of the possible reaction. It is best, however, to address difficulties honestly when they occur. You can always say something like the following:

- 'I have just realised that I gave you some information that was incorrect and, because our relationship with you is important, I wanted to put it right.'

- 'As I think back to our negotiation last week I am concerned that I might have been too aggressive and I want to talk about it so that it does not negatively impact our relationship.'

There is no substitute for being honest!

brilliant exercise

Consider your customer relationships and the situations that can arise where a problem, or 'pinch', could occur. Complete the following table:

Possible problem or 'pinch' point	What can I do to prevent it occurring?	What can I do to solve it appropriately if it does occur?

brilliant recap

Managing the customer relationship is critical if you are to secure more business from a customer in the future.

- Before you can manage a relationship you need to define, specifically, what relationship you want with your customers.
- You must avoid making assumptions about the relationship that exists – you need to be objective about where you are right now with the customer.
- Relationship management is an important (not urgent) task and you need to be proactive.

- Setting objective goals for the relationship is critical to moving it forward.
- Increasing the quality and depth of the relationship is an effective way of building barriers to competitors within your customers.
- You need to deal appropriately with difficulties in a relationship to avoid these 'stacking up' and damaging the relationship.

In managing the customer relationship we have found that there is a lot that you can do. There are a few key priorities that, if you make the time to focus on them, are likely to have a disproportionately positive impact.

Your priorities in managing customers

We have talked in the previous chapter about the need to take proactive action to develop customer relationships, and the principles of being proactive, setting relationship goals and considering different relationship levels. But what are some of our tactical priorities in managing our customers? What are some of the things that we can do quickly and easily? How does managing our customers differ from managing relationships?

Before we give you some of our ideas, think about your own experience.

---

brilliant exercise

Think of times when you have bought something and been delighted by the 'customer experience'. You were made to feel special or, at the very least, the salesperson was focused on the relationship rather than simply the product sale.

What did they do that made you feel special or feel that there was a focus on the relationship?

How, specifically, did it make you feel?

It may be difficult to separate the idea of managing customers (often 'task' -based and about the company) from managing relationships ('people' -based and about individuals). Most good customer management benefits the relationship, and vice versa. Our priorities in managing customers are quite simple but are often not done by salespeople. Whatever our own motivation, we need to think about customer management from the perspective of what our customer wants from us.

> *'A customer is the most important visitor on our premises; he is not dependent on us. We are dependent on him. He is not an interruption in our work. He is the purpose of it. He is not an outsider in our business. He is part of it. We are not doing him a favour by serving him. He is doing us a favour by giving us an opportunity to do so.'* – Mahatma Gandhi, Indian political and ideological leader

Managing our customers starts from the moment that we get the order, but there are different 'categories' that our activities can be divided into. This chapter looks at each of the main categories of activity and gives you some top tips and priorities for each one.

Using the customer as a resource

A customer is a valuable resource to you, and not just because they have paid for a product or service that you have provided. You can utilise their decision to purchase in a number of ways to help you increase your business. As part of your management of the customer you need to consider how you can maximise the benefit of their becoming a customer of yours.

A customer can:

- **Act as a reference**: either with a written testimonial or on the telephone with prospects.
- **Be the subject of a case study**: you can use case studies as marketing and sales collateral and to help other prospects

in a similar situation understand the real benefits of working with your product/service and with you as a company.

- **Give you referrals to other potential customers**: your customer probably knows other people who could benefit from your product or service and can give you their names.

Interestingly, asking customers to act as a reference or give you referrals actually increases their sense of loyalty towards you as a supplier. By agreeing to do either of these things, the customer is 'putting their name' to your product and company. This makes them more likely to tell others about it and to speak positively about you (as long as you give a good service and your product does what it says!).

the time to ask for referrals is at the peak of the customer's gratitude curve

When should you ask?

There is something called a 'gratitude curve' (created by a lawyer, Jay Foonberg), and the time to ask for referrals is when your customer is at the peak of their gratitude curve. This might be at the time of purchase by the customer or, if your product delivers value after a period of time, it might be at the point that the customer realises the value, so you need to think about it. For example, I had an amazing meal recently that was at a table situated in the middle of the kitchen of the restaurant. It was eight courses, and you interacted with the chef. At the point when I had finished the meal, would I have been prepared to write a brief testimonial or tell my friends? Absolutely!

When we have delivered some training or consulting work that has made a positive difference to the customer, we have a habit of asking for the names of two or three people that we might contact and introduce our services to, mentioning their name as an existing customer. If you do a good job, people will be pleased to give you names.

brilliant tips

1. Identify, for your product or service, when the customer is likely to be at the peak of their gratitude curve.
2. List all the ways in which you could utilise this.

Adding value to the customer – constantly

I recently had an experience of a service provider adding real value. I had purchased a new TV and amplifier system and this person, Luke, was coming to install and set the system up for me. When Luke arrived, the first thing he did was lay a sheet out over the floor to prevent any dust or dirt from his work getting on the furniture or carpet – a good start. After a while he popped his head round my office door and asked if I had a TV in any other room and then promptly proceeded to connect this up to the same system, giving me satellite TV access from one dish and without me spending any more money. His retort when I mentioned this was simply 'Well, it's no problem and I thought you might find it useful'. Ten minutes after he had finished and left the house I was 'testing' my new system with a very loud music DVD and the DVD player gave a clunk and stopped working. Luke was back in less than 30 minutes, found that it was a hardware problem (beyond the scope of his services) and got me up and running with a replacement DVD player on a loan basis – I had not even purchased the original player from him!

I have recommended Luke to lots of people, and am even mentioning him in this book! He now has access to a wide network of people that a) he would not have been connected to ordinarily, and b) he is not even aware of (until one of them calls him 'out of the blue'). That is the power of adding value to your customers.

'We see our customers as invited guests to a party, and we are the hosts. It's our job every day to make every important aspect of the customer experience a little bit better.' – Jeff Bezos, US founder of Amazon.com

By adding value whenever you can, you build trust. Here are some ways in which you can add value. They are just examples:

by adding value whenever you can, you build trust

- Send information that allows your customers to be better educated about their market – press cuttings, latest research, the competition to their company.
- Demonstrate how they can make more money in a new way.
- Demonstrate how they can save money.
- Send something for free that may have a high perceived value.
- Think about educating them in every face to face meeting.
- Offer training to the staff.
- Invite them to a networking event.

And, if you want to know what you could do that would *really* add value to the customer, you could just ask: 'What could I do that would add most value going forward?'.

Customer knowledge and understanding

Part of your ongoing management of your customers has to be to get as clear a picture as possible of their organisation as it relates to your product or service offering. You need to:

- Understand the challenges and priorities they face in their market.
- Broaden your contact base within the customer – identify decision makers and influencers, get introductions to them.

- Understand the culture and how decisions are made.
- Understand the personal wins and motivations for the key contacts you have.
- Find out what is happening in the business that might represent more opportunity for you.
- Research them using tools such as the internet so that you are aware of changes that could help or hinder you, and can be proactive in adding value through your business-focused conversations with them.
- Speak to others who might have connections with the customer (other suppliers, for example) to increase your knowledge.

brilliant tip

One of the easiest and most effective ways of increasing customer knowledge and understanding is by spending time with the customer. Look for opportunities – formally and socially if appropriate – to meet and ask questions.

General good practice

Here are some general 'good practice' tips. Most take very little time to do and have a disproportionate benefit. All of these are proactive and important (never urgent) tasks, and so the challenge is for you to make the time to do them.

Welcome new customers

Get the relationship off to a good start by formally welcoming the customer where appropriate. This might be with a small welcome gift, a letter outlining your commitment or something else that makes them feel valued. And, no, this is not the same as sending your standard terms and conditions of sale! To find out more about welcome packs, read the article contained in the free resource pack that accompanies this book (email **resources@brilliant-selling.com** to receive this pack).

Expectations meetings

Once a contract has been signed, and especially where you will be interacting a lot with the customer around the delivery of the product or service, it is often beneficial to have an expectations meeting. The details of a working relationship between customer and supplier are often not discussed explicitly and this makes it more likely for one or other party not to meet the other's expectations. Having an explicit conversation around how the relationship and interaction will work is well suited to a consultative sales approach and can head off possible difficulties before they occur. Also, once you have had a conversation about, for example, how quickly you will respond to telephone messages, it makes it easier to refer to these agreed standards and expectations when a difficulty does arise.

Examples of topics to include in an expectations meeting are:

- How you will communicate – how often, telephone, face to face, etc.
- Agreement to raise problems immediately they occur.
- What you will deliver, specifically.
- What you need from the customer, specifically.
- Agreement to review how the relationship is going.

Immediate follow-up

Get into the habit of following up meetings or telephone calls immediately. The follow-up could be as simple as confirming a meeting and outline agenda following a telephone call, or emailing the customer your understanding of the actions and timescales following a meeting you attended.

Account planning

The specifics of this will vary widely depending on your circumstances, but it is always good practice to have a plan. Without an account plan you lack direction and focus. If you need to interact with other people in your company in order to sell, then a clear plan helps them see where you are headed and their part in the bigger picture.

At its most basic, an account plan needs to consider what your goal is with the customer over what period of time, along with the key actions that you need to take. More comprehensive account plans might include information about the following:

- Contact details for influencers and decision makers in the account.
- How each of them feels about your company.
- Individual action plans to influence decision makers.
- Information about the client and their priorities and challenges.

brilliant tip

The free resource pack accompanying this book contains examples of account planning templates to give you ideas of what you need to focus on. Email **resources@brilliant-selling.com** to receive your copy.

Staying in touch

Although it is good common sense to stay in touch with your customers, we often do not do this as regularly as we should. As long as the relationship is built on us adding value, the customer is unlikely to object to staying in touch and it is important that our customers know that we are thinking of them. There are a number of ways of doing this other than the 'I'm just calling to stay in touch' approach. Here are some ways you can stay in touch with your customers:

- Send them a newsletter.
- Have formal meetings.
- Invite them for a drink or to a social or corporate event.
- Invite them to a networking opportunity.
- Give them a call on the telephone ('I just saw something in this month's … and thought you might be interested …').
- Send magazine or web articles that might be of value or interest to them.
- Send them a birthday card.
- Inform them of changes in policy or management.
- Give them an opportunity to meet your boss.
- Call them to make sure they received the order, and find out what they thought.

Meeting management

Meetings represent a significant investment in your time (especially if you have to travel to the customer) and we must take responsibility for making the most of this investment by following some simple but important points:

- When you arrange a meeting, make sure you propose an agenda and give the customer an opportunity to comment on it. This shows you are interested, professional and keen to maximise the use of time.
- Always confirm a meeting by email – especially if it has been arranged a long time in advance.
- Think about ways in which you can add value in every meeting.

- When the meeting starts, clarify that the agenda is still appropriate and the amount of time you have for the meeting.
- Be clear on the desired outcome or objective for a meeting. This focuses the participants on achieving it and helps prevent a meeting drifting off track.
- Summarise the actions, responsibilities and timelines at the end of the meeting and confirm by email.

brilliant recap

Managing your customers effectively need not take up lots of time. There are some priorities, and in this section we have focused on the following key points:

- Always consider how you can utilise the customer as a resource through referrals, references and case studies.
- Constantly look for ways to add value to the customer.
- Take time to increase your knowledge of the customer, their issues and your contacts within the company.
- Make sure you stay in touch with your customers.

Have a plan for the customer – know where you want to get to with them!

Summary – your brilliant future

It has been quite a journey!

You may have read the whole book (if so, we are impressed with your dedication) or you may have dipped into sections, which we hope have offered new insights. Reading this book may have stimulated your thinking about how to Sell Brilliantly. We are at the end point. However, your learning journey may have only just begun! We have told you what we think, we have asked you to get involved, we have focused on the practicalities of selling and now it is over to you again. Are you someone with good intentions or do you take action when you know it makes sense?

Most of you will have been on a training course at some point in your career and will be familiar with the typical ending – creating an action plan. The truth is that without positive action this book will soon become a distant memory (only after, of course, you have told all your friends about it).

> *'If you always do what you've always done, you'll always get what you always got.'* – NLP presupposition

Do you want to get even better results? Do you understand the importance of executing on new ideas as soon as possible? If so, take some time to reflect now …

Below is a reminder of what we have covered. As you look back now on the content of *Brilliant Selling*, identify the three core areas on which you want to focus.

Part 1: You

- The personality of a salesperson.
- How values and beliefs impact sales success.
- Your personal 'brand'.
- Performance and selling.
- Continually improving through self-coaching.

Part 2: Process and planning

- The sales process as a tool for improvement.
- Making the most of your time.
- Planning for success.
- Setting the right goals.
- Managing sales information.

Part 3: Your power to influence

- The C3 model – the foundations of effective influencing.
- Asking the right questions.
- Listening and learning.
- Negotiating collaboratively.

Part 4: Understanding buyers and prospects

- How do you sell?
- The modern buyer.
- Prospecting with purpose.
- Initial meeting(s) with the prospect.
- Identifying what the prospect wants and needs.

Part 5: Presenting solutions

- Appealing to the customer.
- Writing great sales proposals.
- Preparing winning pitches.

- Persuasive delivery.
- Making the most of objections.
- Closing and commitment.

Part 6: Developing customers

- The value of a customer.
- Managing the relationship.
- Your priorities in managing customers.

---

brilliant exercise

Grab a pen right now and answer these questions for each of the three areas you have nominated:

- What in particular did you find useful about this part?
- How can you start applying these learning points to your current role?
- What are you going to do in the next four weeks?
- What are you going to do tomorrow?
- How will you know you have made the changes you want to make?

Go out there and make a difference. If you need more support then visit us at **www.brilliant-selling.com**. If you want to look at our sales resource library then email us RIGHT NOW at **resources@brilliant-selling.com**. We are keen to find out how this book has helped you specifically. Please send your stories, anecdotes and experiences to us at **info@brilliant-selling.com**. Enjoy the ride – you have what it takes to be a Brilliant Salesperson!

And finally, a story …

Some years ago now, there lived an ambitious young artist. He lived in a small village on the edge of a narrow valley. Often, he would gather his materials up and clamber to the top of the nearest hill and, from the shade of a large oak tree, survey all that was in front of him. He spent hours up there, under the same comfortable tree, painting and contemplating. He thought about who he was and what he could become. He practised painting – in oil, water-colour and pencil. He worked hard to notice the shape and outline of his village in different lights as the seasons changed inexorably around him. He found that the more he practised, the better he got. He noticed that if he took the time to plan his vision in detail, the pictures were richer and more evocative.

Word soon spread, and within a few short years he had a strong following in the local community. He cultivated good relations with all who were interested in his work, and he became celebrated as an expert on the local landscape. He began to make good money from his work and noticed that the better he became, the less he had to bargain. He was delighted that some of his patrons wanted to buy more of his work, and he listened carefully and asked questions to discover what they particularly had in mind.

He began to exhibit his work in a local gallery and was careful to create a special space so that his paintings were shown at their best. Locals and many others from further afield came and were impressed with his versatility and craftsmanship and the careful and subtle way he framed his pictures.

One beautiful autumn day some years later, when the shade from the oak tree that sheltered his position on the hillside was lengthening and he was finishing a commission, he thought about what he wanted to do next. He was restless. He knew in his heart of hearts that to improve as an artist he would have to leave the safety of the valley and expand his horizons. He resolved that this was the next stage in his journey. So the very next day, having thanked his patrons and promising to keep in touch, he set off for the next valley and the valley beyond. Over the years he continued to improve and his skills were noticed by more and more people. As he travelled, the richness of his paintings was matched by the wealth in his pocket. But he always remembered that his artistic journey started in a small village on the edge of a narrow valley, under the shade of that old oak tree.

Index